D1362321

COGNITIVE STYLES: ESSENCE AND ORIGINS

COGNITIVE STYLES: ESSENCE AND ORIGINS

FIELD DEPENDENCE AND FIELD INDEPENDENCE

HERMAN A. WITKIN
and
DONALD R. GOODENOUGH

Psychological Issues
Monograph 51

INTERNATIONAL UNIVERSITIES PRESS, INC.
New York

Library of Congress Cataloging in Publication Data

Witkin, Herman A
Cognitive styles, essence and origins.

(Psychological issues; monograph 51)
Bibliography: p.
Includes indexes.
1. Cognitive styles. 2. Field dependence
(Psychology) I. Goodenough, Donald R., 1927–
joint author. II. Title. III. Series.
BF311.W5948 1981 155.2'3 80-39995
ISBN 0-8236-1003-9

Grateful acknowledgment is made to the publisher for permission to quote from the following: *Four Quartets,* by T. S. Eliot. By permission of Harcourt Brace Jovanovich, Inc.

CONTENTS

Acknowledgments vii

Herman A. Witkin (1916–1979) ix

Introduction 1

1 Historical Development of the Concepts of Field Dependence-Independence and Psychological Differentiation 7

2 Field Dependence Revisited 23

3 Origins of the Field-Dependent and Field-Independent Cognitive Styles 65

References 103

Name Index 127

Subject Index 135

About the Authors 143

ACKNOWLEDGMENTS

For their helpful comments on sections of earlier versions of this monograph we are indebted to John Berry, J. Kent Davis, Walter Emmerich, Sidney Irvine, Samuel Messick, Philip K. Oltman, Juan Pascual-Leone, Ype H. Poortinga, and Joseph R. Royce. The preparation of this monograph was aided by a grant (MH-21989) from the National Institute of Mental Health.

Herman A. Witkin

HERMAN A. WITKIN
(1916–1979)

With great sadness we report the death of Herman A. Witkin while this monograph was in press.

Professor Witkin received his Ph.D. from New York University in 1939, taught at Brooklyn College from 1940 to 1952, served as Professor with the Department of Psychiatry of the State University of New York Downstate Medical Center from 1952 to 1971, and came to Educational Testing Service in 1971. In 1976 he was appointed Distinguished Research Scientist at ETS, where he remained until his death on July 8, 1979.

He was a world-renowned investigator of cognitive styles as integrative processes in personality development. His research on cognitive styles began in the 1940s with the now-classical studies of individual differences in perception of the upright in space. His pursuit of the significance of individual differences in cognitive processes remained central throughout his career. This unifying interest, however, led him into extraordinarily diverse domains of psychology, including the study of dreaming, of socialization processes across cultures, of relations between teacher and student, patient and therapist, parent and child, and of the effect of chromosomal aberrations on human behavior. This wide range of experimental approaches, linked through a common theoretical framework, marked his style as a scientist.

Professor Witkin lived to see his life's work achieve the recognition it so clearly deserves. The many tributes to his accomplishments include an honorary doctor of social sciences degree from Tilburg University in The Netherlands at a ceremony attended by Queen Juliana in 1977.

Professor Witkin published numerous books and articles on the field-dependence-independence cognitive-style dimension, including two landmark volumes, *Personality Through Perception: An Experimental and Clinical Study* in 1954, and *Psychological Differentiation: Studies of Development* in 1962. The cumulative impact of these publications is illustrated by the fact that he is included among the 100 most cited authors in the *Social Sciences Citation Index*.

Field-dependence theory was, for Witkin, an ever changing structure. During the long history of his work he periodically redefined and extended the conceptual framework to incorporate new data and newly emerging insights. The present monograph describes the last of his periodic reintegrations of theory and data concerning the nature and origins of the field-dependence-independence cognitive-style dimension. Just before his death, Professor Witkin wrote the following: "Though it has changed very much in its lifetime, field-dependence theory is still very much in evolution. We can therefore be quite sure that, just as it has changed in the past, it will appear quite different in the future under the impetus of newly emerging evidence. An evolving theory is inevitably characterized by lacunae and uncertainties. This is surely true of field-dependence theory at this moment. These lacunae and uncertainties in themselves provided an impetus for research which can serve to advance the theory." It was his hope that this monograph might stimulate such research.

Donald R. Goodenough

INTRODUCTION

1979 was the 30th anniversary of the public inaugural of the New Look movement in perception. The inaugural event was a symposium on "Personal and Social Factors in Perception," held at the annual meeting of the American Psychological Association. By that time, of course, the research that bore the New Look label was already in full swing. It was in the New Look movement that cognitive-style research had its beginnings and its earliest intellectual base.

Participants in the New Look movement were a loose confederation of psychologists critical of the dominant approaches to perception then in vogue. Diverse as they were in their particular criticisms, their shared discontent was that these approaches neglected the person who does the perceiving. That discontent was epitomized by the title of a paper by Klein and Schlesinger (1949) given at the symposium: "Where Is the Perceiver in Perceptual Theory?" In the New Look view it is not enough to examine a given act of perceiving across persons A, B, and C. The act of perceiving in person A also needs to be examined in relation to A's personality structure, A's needs, and A's interests and values. Such an approach inevitably draws attention to the adaptive role of perceiving in the psychological economy of the individual.

Perception psychologists provided only one of the important stimuli for the New Look movement. An additional stimulus was provided by personality psychologists asking a variant of the Klein-Schlesinger question: "Where is perceiving in personality theory?" Developments in psychoanalytic theory made their contribution as well. Ego psychology, particularly in its conception of the conflict-free ego sphere, sought to dissociate perceptual and cognitive functions from the instinctual drives, thereby stressing the biologically adaptive aspects of such functions. All these concerns generated a good deal of intellectual ferment about the nature of perception-personality relationships.

The New Look movement was responsible for a flood of research and publications. The proceedings of the 1949 symposium, with several papers in the same idiom added, were published in a book, *Perception and Personality* (Bruner and Krech, 1950). Soon after came other books, similar in title and in the issues with which they were concerned. One of these was *Perception: An Approach to Personality* (Blake and Ramsey, 1951); another, *Personality Through Perception* (Witkin, Lewis, Hertzman, Machover, Meissner, and Wapner, 1954; hereafter, Witkin et al., 1954). Still later there appeared two major reports in the present monograph series (Gardner, Holzman, Klein, Linton, and Spence, 1959; Gardner, Jackson, and Messick, 1960). Considered in these volumes, and in a host of journal articles, were phenomena as diverse as perceptual defense, subliminal perception, needs and perception, sensory-tonic effects, and individual differences in perceiving.

It was out of the individual-differences tributary of this broad stream of research that there emerged what came to be called cognitive styles by some, including ourselves, and cognitive controls by others, particularly the Menninger group, which reserved the label cognitive styles for patterns of controls. The aim of this research was not to enlarge the catalogue of individual differences on record. Rather, individual differences in perception were to be used as points of departure for inquiry into the broad modes of personal functioning of which they were conceived to be an expression. The initial observation of these differences, and their further study, commonly took place in the laboratory. This feature had important consequences for the products that emerged from cognitive-style research, setting them off from those typical of a psychometric approach to individual differences. Among the cognitive styles identified and investigated in the early New Look days were constricted-flexible control, leveling-sharpening, equivalence range, tolerance for unrealistic experiences, on all of which the Menninger group did pioneer work, and field dependence-independence, on which we ourselves worked. Among later entries have been reflection-impulsivity, conceptualizing, and strong-vs.-weak automatization.

Klein and Schlesinger (1949), in the paper cited, pointed out that a good deal of the New Look work of the time was in fact limited to part-relationships. "Press the button, 'hunger,'" as they put it, "and out comes a perceptual effect." By making the person simply a passageway for linking input (hunger) and outcome (percept) the main point of the New Look movement was not taken, they argued. What Klein and Schlesinger called for instead was assignment of a pivotal role in conceptualizing perception-personality relationships to a central adapting, regulating personality structure, which enters into all functioning, including perceiving. In our current view of field dependence-independence as an expression of the extent of differentiation of an individual's psychological structure we take precisely this stance.

Of the cognitive styles that have been identified, field dependence-independence has received the greatest research attention over the years. There is evidence throughout this monograph of the wide scope of the work that has been done on this dimension. The reasons for the greater research investment in field dependence-independence over other cognitive styles are numerous and diverse. Among these reasons are the demonstrated breadth of the dimension and its evident representation in everyday life, so that its manifestations are salient, "real," and often directly visible; the existence of effective procedures for its assessment, derived from the early extensive laboratory research on the perceptual functions in which individual differences in field dependence-independence express themselves; and the availability of a theoretical framework that makes it possible to bring together a wide variety of psychological phenomena and functions often considered apart from one another.

As noted, we consider field dependence-independence to be an expression of psychological differentiation; field-dependence theory thus has its conceptual home in the larger theory of psychological differentiation. Since differentiation theory was proposed more than a decade and a half ago (Witkin, Dyk, Faterson, Goodenough, and Karp, 1962; hereafter, Witkin et al.,

1962), a very large body of research bearing on it has been reported in the literature.[1] A good deal of that research has been devoted to its field-dependence-independence component. In this monograph we review the newer knowledge on field dependence-independence and propose revisions and extensions of field-dependence theory in light of that knowledge. We recently performed a similar task for the broader theory of psychological differentiation (Witkin, Goodenough, and Oltman, 1979). We consider differentiation theory here only to the extent necessary for our examination of field dependence-independence.

In the new look we now take at field dependence-independence, we repeat a step we have taken at intervals in the past when newly accumulated evidence required and allowed theory revisions and advances. The present visit, as we shall see, uncovers quite extensive changes in field-dependence theory, reflecting the accelerated rate of research on field dependence-independence in the immediate past. We are confident that the process of conceptual change will go on as the evidence continues to grow. This is the way with programmatic research. Phenomena observed long ago acquire a new aspect when they are seen in a fresh theoretical perspective and are linked to other phenomena with which they were not previously connected. It is perhaps as T. S. Eliot put it in his *Four Quartets:* ". . . the end of all our exploring/Will be to arrive where we started/And know the place for the first time."

A second major task of this monograph is to review the evidence on the origins of the field-dependent and field-independent cognitive styles. For this purpose we examine such diverse influences as genetic and endocrine factors, special training, child-rearing, and cultural and ecological effects. We also consider the implications for field-dependence theory of the manner in which differences in cognitive style arise.

While the focus of this monograph is on field dependence-independence, what we have learned about that dimension may tell us much about the essence of cognitive styles in general.

[1]For recent bibliographies, see Cox and Witkin (1978); Witkin, Cox, and Friedman (1976); Witkin, Cox, Friedman, Hrishikesan, and Siegel (1974); Witkin, Oltman, Cox, Ehrlichman, Hamm, and Ringler (1973).

The influences contributing to the development of cognitive styles may indeed be different from one style to another. Yet, the classes of factors that have been identified as important in the development of field dependence and field independence, even if not the specific content of these classes, may suggest useful "places to look" in the search for the origins of individual differences in other cognitive styles.

We begin our examination of the field-dependent and field-independent cognitive styles with an account of the evolution of the field-dependence-independence and differentiation concepts.

1

HISTORICAL DEVELOPMENT OF THE CONCEPTS OF FIELD DEPENDENCE-INDEPENDENCE AND PSYCHOLOGICAL DIFFERENTIATION

Our program of research had its origins in laboratory studies of perception of the upright (Asch and Witkin, 1948a, 1948b; Witkin, 1948, 1949, 1950b, 1952; Witkin and Asch, 1948a, 1948b). In the very earliest studies we sought to determine how people locate the upright as quickly and accurately as they ordinarily do. Beyond contributing to that goal, these studies revealed—quite unexpectedly—that subjects were markedly different from one another in their performance on the orientation tasks we used; and they were self-consistent in manner of establishing the upright across tasks. This suggested that people have preferred ways of integrating the diverse sources of information available to them for locating the upright. Thus, if a full understanding of perception of the upright was to be achieved, these characteristic modes of information processing had to be taken into account, along with field factors and local sensory factors. It seemed to us that a useful route for determining just what it is about the perceiver that matters in the act of perception would be to examine the nature and basis of self-consistency in performance across these orientation tasks and across other tasks as well, to which they might also be related. Although individual differences continued to be of central concern in our subsequent work, that focus was adopted for the sake of achieving a fuller understanding of space orientation, rather than to devise still another typology.

The theoretical framework that progressively emerged in the

further development of the program of research represents successive attempts to conceptualize, first, the early observed self-consistent individual differences in mode of orientation, and, later, the ever-broadening patterns of individual differences identified in subsequent studies of the scope of these self-consistencies. Through the continuous interplay between theory and the products of the empirical effort it stimulated, the conceptualization has eventually been broadened to include personality structure and its development.

Field Dependence and Field Independence as the Tendencies to Use Body or Field as Referents for Perception of the Upright

The direction of the perceived upright is ordinarily determined by two sets of experiences working in tandem. First, the field around us, apprehended through vision, usually has the character of a framework, the main axes of which correspond to the true vertical and horizontal directions of space. This framework provides one ready basis for establishing the upright. Second, the direction of gravity, apprehended through the vestibular, tactile, and kinesthetic senses, provides another definition of the vertical direction of space. Since the upright indicated by the external field and the upright indicated by the gravitational pull coincide in direction, the outcome is the same whether either determinant alone or both in combination are used as referents.

One research strategy we adopted in seeking to understand the basis of perception of the upright was to separate these two standards experimentally. This separation was accomplished in two situations—the body-adjustment test (BAT) and the rod-and-frame test (RFT)—by tilting the visual framework and leaving the gravitational pull on the body unaltered. In another situation—the rotating-room test (RRT)—the separation was accomplished in an opposite manner—by altering the direction of the force acting on the body, while the visual framework remained upright. With both types of change, reliance on the external visual framework results in a different location of the upright than use of the posturally experienced gravitational upright. It is this feature of the tasks that first exposed the existence of individual differences in manner of perceiving the upright, differences which are of course not detectable under everyday circumstances where the two referents coincide in direction.

In the BAT, the subject was seated in a small tilted room that could be displaced clockwise or counterclockwise; his own chair could be displaced by the experimenter in a similar fashion, independently of the room (see Figure 1). When given the task of adjusting the chair (and therefore his own body) from an initially tilted position to the upright, with the surrounding room in a tilted position, some subjects aligned the body with the tilted room, and in that position reported that they were sitting perfectly straight. Clearly, such subjects were using the external visual field as the primary referent for perception of the upright, essentially to the exclusion of sensations from the body. At the opposite extreme of the performance range were subjects who brought the body close to the true (gravitational) upright. It seemed equally evident that for these subjects it was the body which served as the primary referent for perception of the upright. Most subjects brought their bodies to a position somewhere between these two extremes.

In the RFT, the subject was seated in a totally darkened room and viewed a tilted luminous square frame, within which was a luminous rod, pivoted at the same center as the frame, which could be tilted separately from the frame (see Figure 2). The subject's task was to adjust the rod to the upright while the frame remained in its initial position of tilt. Though here it was the position of an external object (the rod) in space, rather than the position of the body itself, that had to be determined, an opportunity was again provided the subject to use body or field as referents. And here again, people differed markedly in the extent to which they relied on one or the other referent.

In the RRT, it was the direction of the force on the body that was changed while the visual field remained upright. This relationship was achieved by seating the subject in a chair, which could be tilted left or right, within a small upright room driven around a circular track, so that the direction of the effective force on the body was the result of the outwardly-acting centrifugal pull and the downward pull of gravity (see Figure 3). As

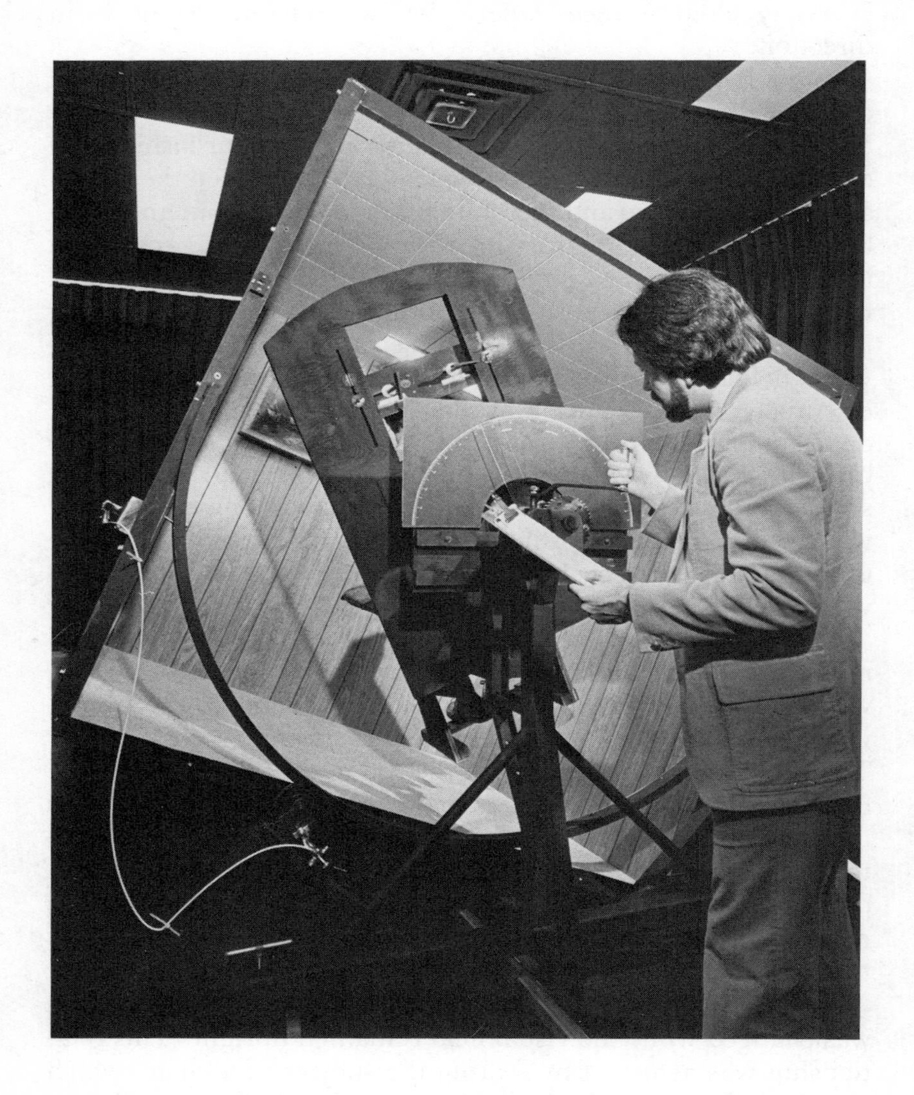

FIGURE 1. The Body-Adjustment Test.

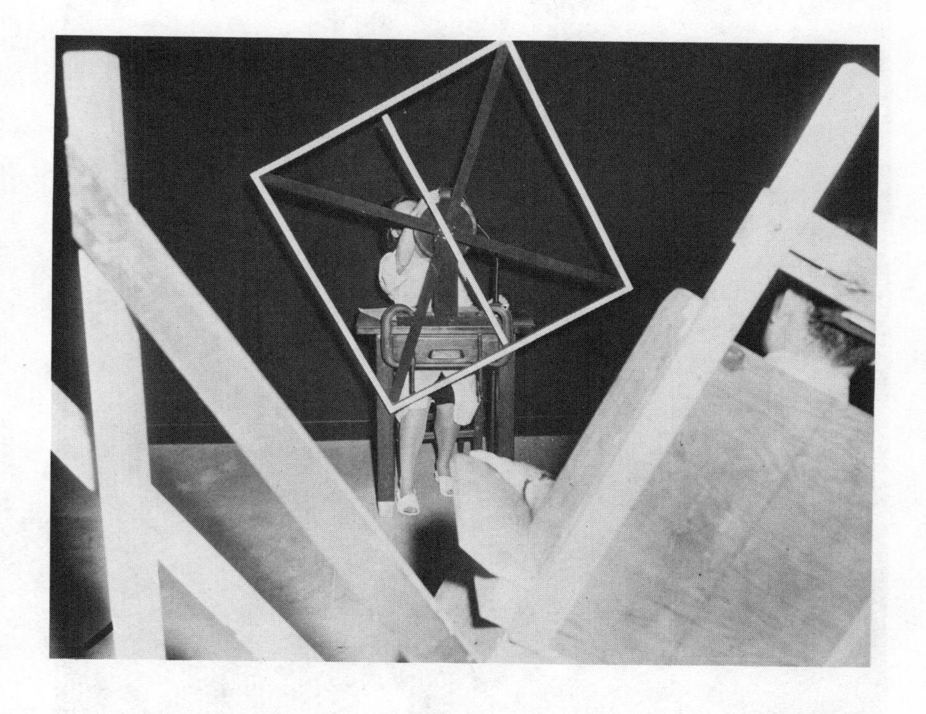

FIGURE 2. The Rod-and-Frame Test. (From: *Personality Through Perception* by H. A. Witkin, H. B. Lewis, M. Hertzman, K. Machover, P. B. Meissner, & S. Wapner. Copyright 1954 by Harper & Brothers. Reprinted by permission.)

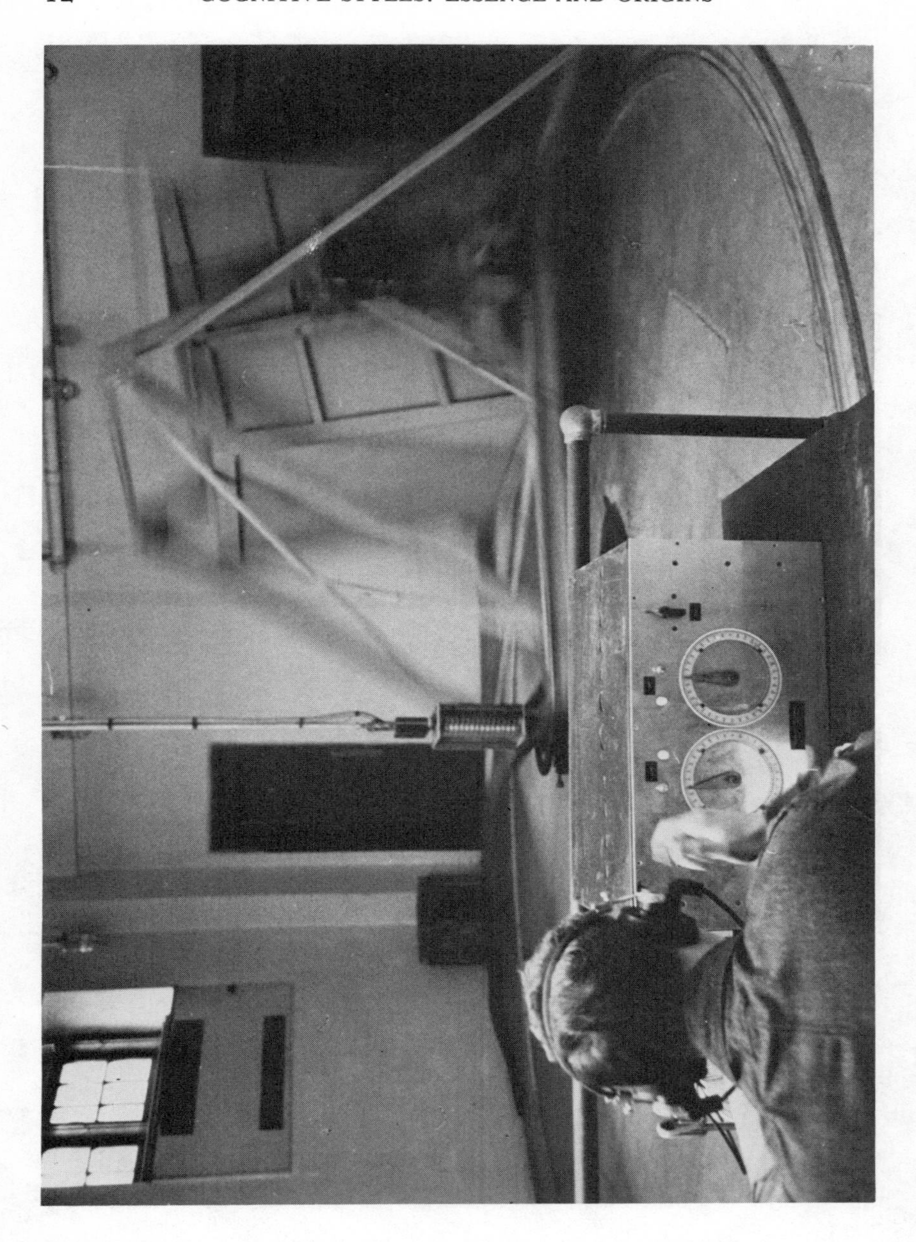

FIGURE 3. The Rotating-Room Test. (From: *Personality Through Perception* by H. A. Witkin, H. B. Lewis, M. Hertzman, K. Machover, P. B. Meissner, & S. Wapner. Copyright 1954 by Harper & Brothers. Reprinted by permission.)

in the BAT, the subject was required to bring his body to a position where he experienced it as straight. In carrying out this task, subjects once more were found to be different in the extent to which they aligned their bodies with the upright room or according to the altered force acting upon them.

Particularly influential in suggesting that the individual differences found in the three situations were to be taken seriously was the later finding that, when subjects were tested in all of them, they tended to be self-consistent with regard to degree of reliance on external field or body. Thus, the subject who tilted his body far toward the tilted room in the BAT was also likely to tilt the rod far toward the tilted frame in the RFT and to align his body with the upright room in the RRT. Conversely, the subject who brought his body close to the true upright in the BAT, regardless of room position, was also likely to separate rod from frame in the RFT and adjust the rod close to the upright; and he was also likely to tilt his body toward alignment with the displaced force acting on it in the RRT.

In our earliest attempt to conceptualize these self-consistent individual differences, several hypotheses were considered and rejected when the experimental evidence failed to support them. The hypothesis we settled on as most consistent with the evidence then available, and as having the greatest heuristic value in guiding further research, was that the individual differences we had observed represented differences in the tendency to use the external visual field or the body itself as a primary referent for perception of the upright. This hypothesis was supported by the observation made in several studies that manipulating the salience of the visual field or of postural cues influenced degree of reliance on field or body as referents for perception of the upright. In one study with the BAT apparatus, postural cues were strengthened by removing the pads that ordinarily covered the seat of the subject's chair; and the structure of the visual field was weakened by using a cylindrical room instead of the normal square room and by reducing the number of vertical and horizontal lines on the front wall facing the subject. Under these conditions, the body was adjusted substantially closer to the true upright than under the standard BAT conditions (Witkin, 1948). In another set of studies, the average displacement of the rod toward the axes of a tilted field increased progressively with three fields of increasing articulation: the luminous frame of the RFT, a small plywood room, and a laboratory scene reflected in a tilted mirror (Asch and Witkin, 1948a, 1948b; Witkin and Asch, 1948b). Taken together with the evidence already reviewed, these observations suggested that individual differences in performance on the RFT, BAT, and RRT were due to differences in extent of reliance on impressions from the body or on the axes of the visual field in determining the upright.

The concept that contrasting modes of establishing the upright reflected primary reference to the external field or to the body, made "field dependent" and "field independent" appropriate designations for these modes. At the time these labels were adopted, our observations were still limited to the orientation tasks, so that the labels were intended to refer quite literally to extent of reliance on visual field or body in perception of the upright. To the extent that scores from each of the three orientation tests formed a continuous distribution, field dependence and field independence represented contrasting tendencies to rely primarily on body or field, rather than distinct types of performance.

The results for the three orientation tests, taken together, made it quite clear that primary reliance on the body would lead to a more accurate performance in some situations, whereas reliance on the visual field would lead to a more accurate performance in other situations. Thus, in the RFT and BAT reliance on cues from the body leads to relatively accurate adjustments of rod or body to the gravitational vertical. In the RRT, on the other hand, reliance on bodily cues leads to relatively inaccurate adjustments. Thus, neither a field-dependent nor field-independent mode of functioning is uniformly good or bad in their consequences for perception of the upright in space.

Field Independence as Overcoming Embedding Contexts in Perception

The next major conceptual step we took was stimulated by the results of studies that pursued in other perceptual domains the individual differences first observed in perception of the upright. In these further studies of self-consistency, we considered the possibility that, while the three orientation tasks assessed reliance on field or body, they could also be conceived to involve separation of an item (body or rod) from an organized field (room or frame). This possibility was studied in the context of perceptual tasks that required the subject to disembed an item from an organized field of which it was a part, but that did not involve body-field juxtaposition or perception of the upright. An example of such a task is the embedded-figures test (EFT) (Witkin, 1950a), in which the subject is shown a simple figure and then required to find it in a complex design that is so patterned that each component of the simple figure is made part of a clear-cut subwhole of the pattern; the simple figure is thereby effectively hidden (see Figure 4). To locate the simple figure it is necessary to break up the organized pattern so as to expose the figure. It was found that subjects who had difficulty separating the sought-after simple figure from the complex design were the ones who could not easily keep body or rod separate from room or frame in the orientation tests—in other words, were the ones who were field dependent. Conversely, people who were field independent in the orientation tests found it easy to overcome the influence of the organized complex design in locating the simple figure within it.

These findings, and others as well, suggested that the field-dependence-independence dimension was more general than it had appeared to be when first defined on the basis of data from the orientation tasks alone; and they suggested as well that the more general dimension might be conceived as involving individual differences in ease or difficulty in separating an item from an organized field or overcoming an embedding context (Witkin et al., 1954). Field dependence-independence was thus specifically conceived to be a perceptual-analytical ability that manifests itself pervasively throughout an individual's perceptual functioning.

Articulated-vs.-Global Field Approach

Further studies of the scope of the individual difference in

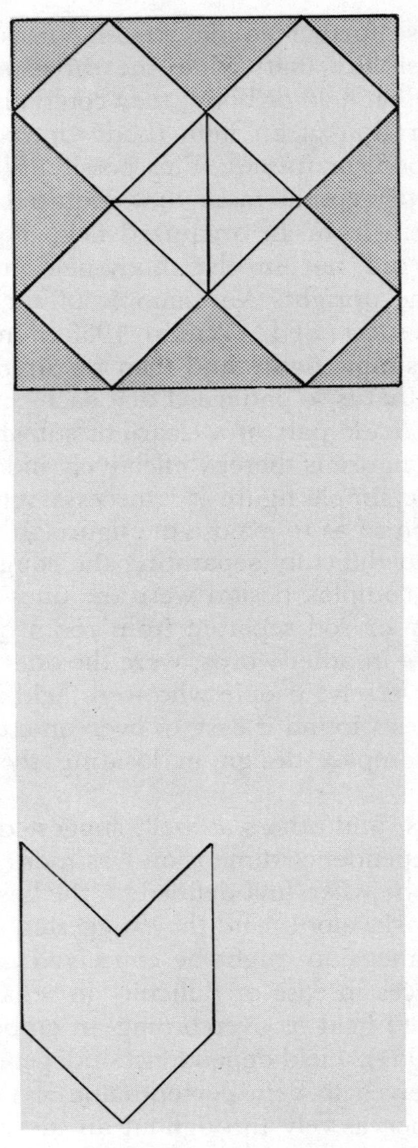

FIGURE 4. Sample of simple and complex figures similar to those used in the Embedded-Figures Test. (From: Witkin, H. A., Moore, C. A., Goodenough, D. R., & Cox, P. W., "Field-Dependent and Field-Independent Cognitive Styles and Their Educational Implications." *Review of Educational Research,* Winter 1977, pp. 1–64. Copyright 1977, American Educational Research Association, Washington, D.C. Reprinted by permission.)

disembedding ability, broadly expressed in perception, focused on two main issues: first, the relation between disembedding ability in perception and disembedding ability in intellectual functioning; and, second, the relation between disembedding ability and structuring ability.

Research on the first issúe was guided by the view that separating a part from the context in which it is embedded is as much a feature of some kinds of problem-solving tasks, where the person deals with symbolic representations, as it is of the kinds of perceptual tasks we had been considering, where the person deals with an immediately present stimulus configuration. Subjects identified as field dependent in perception of the upright were found to have greater difficulty in solving that particular class of problems in which the solution depends on taking an element critical for solution out of the context in which it is presented and restructuring the problem material so that the element is now used in a different context (e.g., Glucksberg, 1956; Harris, cited in Witkin et al. [1962]). Evidence such as this suggested that greater or less disembedding or analytical ability shows itself across an individual's perceptual and intellectual activities.

Research on the second issue—the relation between disembedding and structuring—was stimulated by the view that underlying both is a tendency to deal with the field in a more active or more passive manner. The tendency to leave the stimulus material "as is" or to act upon it (break up the organized pattern so as to expose the embedded figure), as observed in the EFT, may be expected to show itself in congruent fashion when people have to deal with a field that lacks clear inherent organization. The expectation that field-independent people would impose structure on such a field, and therefore experience it as organized, whereas field-dependent people would not, was supported in many studies using both perceptual and problem-solving tasks (Witkin et al., 1962).

The evidence linking field dependence-independence to the ability to overcome embedding contexts in problem-solving tasks and to structuring ability in perceptual and intellectual functioning, substantially broadened the scope of the individual differences we were tracing. To accommodate this expanded picture of self-consistency still another conceptual step was taken. Analysis and structuring were viewed as complementary aspects of articulation. Thus, the person who experiences in articulated fashion can apprehend items as discrete from their backgrounds when the field is organized, and can impose structure on a field when the field has little inherent structure, in this way apprehending the field as organized. The enlarged dimension of individual differences was now conceived as "an articulated field approach" at one extreme and a "global field approach" at the other extreme. The designation "field approach" was used because we seemed to be dealing with characteristic ways of functioning that people bring to situations that call for them.

Psychological Differentiation

Subsequent research linked the individual differences described thus far to differences in a still wider array of areas, including, in particular, areas ordinarily subsumed under personality, such as controls and defenses, body concept, and the self (Witkin et al., 1962; Witkin et al., 1954). When it became clear that these areas could not be accommodated within the articulated-global construct, another theoretical step had to be taken. "Differentiation" recommended itself, on several grounds, as a useful construct for conceptualizing the enlarged picture of self-consistency that had now emerged. First, each of the constituents of the cluster of characteristics found to be associated with one another showed a definite ordering during ontogenetic development. Second, the characteristics that had been implicated were clearly formal rather than content properties of a psychological system—that is, typical ways of functioning based on given structural arrangements. Third, as may be expected of characteristics of a formal nature, they were stable over time. Fourth, common to many of the characteristics was degree of specialization of function; others reflected degree of separateness of the self from the selves of others. All the features listed are in fact distinguishing properties of a relatively more differentiated or less differentiated psychological system, suggesting that the concept of differentiation was a useful one for characterizing commonality among the linked areas of psychological functioning and their common fate during development. Field dependence-independence was accordingly now placed in the broader framework of differentiation (Witkin et al., 1962).

In briefest outline, differentiation is a structural property of an organismic system. Particular formal arrangements, determined by a given degree of differentiation, influence the development of characteristic ways of functioning. In fact, it is through particular functional manifestations that degree of differentiation of a system may be judged.

To characterize a system as more differentiated implies, first of all, segregation of self from nonself, or self-nonself polarity. Boundaries have been formed between an inner core, experienced as the self, and nonself. Boundaries are not as definite in a less differentiated system, where there is greater connectedness with others. Differentiation also implies segregation of psychological activities from each other, as thinking from acting, feeling from perceiving. It means as well specificity of functioning within each activity. The separate, specialized functions that emerge with increasing differentiation do not operate independently of each other. Instead, they are interrelated into a hierarchical structure, making them integral constituents of an articulated system.

Finally, reflecting its organismic character, differentiation implies specialization of function at the neurophysiological level as much as at the psychological level. Just as specialization is taken as an indication of psychological differentiation, specialization of functions in the two cerebral hemispheres serves as an indicator of neurophysiological differentiation.

The position at which we had now arrived was that the components of the different patterns of individual functioning we had identified were in effect diverse expressions of differences in extent of differentiation. A central postulate of the theory of psychological differentiation formulated in 1962 as a guide to further research (Witkin et al., 1962) was that the development of differentiation is an organism-wide process. Accordingly, greater or less differentiation is likely to characterize an individual's functioning in diverse domains. Operationally, this means that manifestations or indicators of greater or less differentiation from each of a number of domains should be related, to some extent, making for self-consistent individual functioning across domains.

Among these indicators (cast in the direction of greater differentiation) was, first of all, an articulated field approach in cognitive functioning, already defined. A second indicator was sense of separate identity, conceived as identification by the individual of attributes, needs, values he recognizes as his own and as distinct from those of others; a developed sense of separate identity allows the individual to function with a degree of autonomy from others. A third indication was an articulated body concept—that is, an impression of the body as having definite limits or boundaries and of the parts within as discrete yet interrelated and formed into a definite structure. The fourth indicator was the availability of structured controls for channeling impulse, and the tendency to use specific defenses, such as intellectualization, isolation, and projection, rather than relatively nonspecific defenses, such as repression and denial. By 1962, the time of our last major statement of differentiation theory (Witkin et al., 1962), there was a good deal of evidence that measures of these various indicators of differentiation were interrelated, as expected. A large body of additional research reported in the literature since then, and recently reviewed by Witkin, Goodenough, and Oltman (1979), has provided further evidence on the interrelatedness of these indicators. The newer work, as we will see later, has also implicated specialization of neurophysiological functions in the network of evidence on differentiation. That indicator of differentiation of the organism had not yet been examined empirically at the time of our 1962 statement of differentiation theory.

A word is in order here about the relationship between differentiation and the other major dimension of development: integration. Consideration of that relationship will help to better define the place of differentiation in the stream of development.

More differentiated systems are likely to be more complexly organized, in the sense that the relations between components of the system and between the system and its environment are more elaborate. On the other hand, there are no grounds for expecting differentiation to be related to effectiveness of integration, in the sense of harmonious relations among system components and between the system and its environment. Consistent with the concept that extent of differentiation is unrelated to effectiveness of integration, numerous studies have shown that more differentiated and less differentiated people are not different in sheer presence or absence of pathology, in other words, in being well adjusted or poorly adjusted (Witkin, 1965). Early studies suggested, however, that the form that psychopathology takes, should it develop, is related to level of differentiation. In particular, the psychopathology found in more differentiated patients appeared to represent exaggerated or bizarre manifestations of the personality functioning found in normal people who are relatively more differentiated; the psychopathology found in less differentiated patients appeared to represent exaggerated or bizarre manifestations of the personality functioning found in normal less differentiated people. From the perspective of differentiation, there thus appeared to be continuity in forms of functioning between relatively normal and relatively pathological people.

These possibilities were suggested by an early in-depth study of a group of hospitalized psychiatric patients by means of intense clinical interviews, the Rorschach, the TAT, and figure drawings (Witkin et al., 1954). To begin with, measures from these various assessment techniques that had earlier been found to relate to the standing of normal people on the differentiation dimension, for the most part also distinguished relatively more differentiated and less differentiated psychiatric patients. Moreover, the clinical characterizations of more differentiated patients included characteristics common among more differentiated people (such as autonomous functioning and developed controls and specialized defenses), while the clinical characterizations of less differentiated patients included characteristics common among normal less differentiated people (such as greater connectedness with others, limited self-reliance, poor control over impulse expression, and use of nonspecific defenses). This becomes evident when we consider the personality characterizations made of male patients, regardless of diagnostic category, at the field-dependent and field-independent extremes in the patient population we studied. Among men in the field-independent group we found expansive, euphoric delusions of grandeur, indicating high apparent self-esteem; arrogant, assaultive, destructive behavior, indicating outward expression of aggression; attempts to maintain masculine identity; projections of guilt, suggesting the preservation of apparent self-esteem; and, in a minority of cases, weak, inadequate selves. Common to most of these constellations is some evidence of struggle for the maintenance of self among people who are conceived to have a delineated self. Among male patients in the field-dependent group we more commonly found uncontrolled acting out of impulses, indicating inadequate control over impulse expression; impulsive arson and eneuresis until adolescence, again indicating problems of impulse control; aggression directed inward, resulting in low self-esteem and narcissistic behavior; open castration wishes, indicating a desire to abandon masculine identity; various forms of passive behavior, including helplessness, weeping, and dependence. This personality constellation gives much less evidence of struggle for maintenance of the self among people conceived to be more connected with others and less autonomous in their functioning.

Since this very early work with hospitalized psychiatric patients, many studies have examined extent of differentiation among patients in a variety of symptom categories. We will not review those studies here, but only note that research on the relation between differentiation and forms of pathology is a promising line of work.

In sum, in the 1962 version of differentiation theory, differentiation served to conceptualize the enlarged picture of self-consistency that had by then emerged. Within that conceptualization, an articulated-vs.-global field approach, our earlier highest-level construct, was regarded as one manifestation of greater or less differentiation; and field dependence-independence referred to a component of that field-approach dimension: greater or less disembedding ability in perceptual functioning.

2

FIELD DEPENDENCE REVISITED

Particularly influential in guiding us from our earlier view of field dependence-independence, described in the preceding pages, to our current conception are two bodies of research carried out since 1962. One is concerned with the articulated-global field-approach dimension, the other with autonomy in social behavior and interpersonal competencies. We turn now to a review of the results of these two streams of research. As we review these results we will take note of the suggestions they offer for theory revision and extension. We will then propose a model of field dependence-independence that seems best to accommodate the newer evidence, and consider the implications of the model for the conception of cognitive styles.

The New Evidence: Cognitive Restructuring

A large body of research since 1962 has been concerned with the hypothesis that there is a general dimension of individual differences that involves articulated-vs.-global cognitive functioning in perceptual and intellectual activities. These studies have linked field independence in perception of the upright to a number of dimensions of cognitive functioning that may be conceived to involve cognitive restructuring ability. Although field-dependent and field-independent people do not appear to differ with regard to the immediate percept induced by most stimuli, field-independent people seem better able to achieve a different percept—when required to do so by situational demands or inner needs—through the restructuring of their initial perceptual experience, at least with respect to spatial-configurational material. In contrast, among field-dependent people the prevailing organization of the perceptual field is likely to be adhered to as given. A difference in restructuring ability between field-dependent and field-independent people, similar to that observed in their perceptual activities, is also evident in their intellectual functioning.

The differentiation concept, which proposes self-consistent functioning across domains as a reflection of extent of differentiation, suggests that an individual would show the same characteristic level of restructuring ability across tasks involving different sense modalities, as well as across tasks featuring spatial material and symbolic material. Most studies of the generality of restructuring ability have used spatial-visual types of material. A few studies have examined restructuring in other media as well. The evidence bearing on the hypothesis that cognitive restructuring ability is a very general competence, related to performance in tests of perception of the upright, is reviewed in the section that follows.

Another body of evidence from research stimulated by the articulated-global construct bears on the nature of the processes involved in tests of perception of the upright. At one point, as noted, we hypothesized that performance on tests of perception of the upright featured disembedding ability. While the newer evidence confirms our earlier view that critical to performance on such tests is extent of reliance on body or visual field as primary referents, it suggests that the processes involved may be distinct from, though related to, those involved in the solution of an embedded-figures problem, which is an exemplar of a cognitive restructuring task. The evidence bearing on the distinctiveness of performance on tests of perception of the upright and on cognitive restructuring tasks is reviewed in the second section below.

Relation between Cognitive Restructuring and Field Independence in Perception of the Upright

Field independence, as manifested by the manner of determining the upright in space, was found in our early studies to be significantly related to ease of locating simple figures in embedding or complex organized gestalten. Successful performance of a disembedding task very clearly requires restructuring of a visual perceptual field. Since the early findings, many other studies have confirmed the relation between RFT performance and disembedding ability in both the visual and tactile modalities (e.g., Dumsha, Minard, and McWilliams, 1973; Pizzamiglio, 1976; Witkin, Goodenough, and Karp, 1967). It is now abundantly clear that field independence in perception of the upright is closely related to a cognitive dimension identified in factor-analytical studies labeled "flexibility of closure" by Thurstone (1944), or "convergent production of figural transformation" by Guilford (1967) (e.g., Bergman and Engelbrektson, 1973; Goodenough and Karp, 1961; McWhinnie, 1970a; Witkin et al., 1962). A variety of embedded-figures tests have high loadings on this factor.

Since 1962 a great deal of evidence has accumulated relating performance on the RFT to other cognitive dimensions that clearly feature spatial restructuring. This evidence is consistent with the hypothesis that field independence in perception of the upright is related to spatial restructuring ability. We list, as illustrative, some of the many cognitive dimensions, in addition to disembedding, that appear to require spatial restructuring and have been related to RFT performance.

Perceptual constancy. Many object properties are relatively invariant in immediate visual perception, despite changes in setting or spatial location that result in very different retinal representations. It is possible, however, to perceive and make judgments about the retinal image, as distinct from the object itself. The evidence suggests that judgments about the appearance of objects are not related to RFT performance, but Linden (1976) has reported that field-independent subjects tend to be more accurate than field-dependent subjects when required to judge properties of the retinal image in a size-constancy situation. The act of perceiving what the retinal image looks like can be described as a restructuring of the immediate object percept. These data are therefore consistent with the view that field independence in perception of the upright is related to restructuring ability.

Speed of closure. Performance on tests of this dimension has been related to RFT performance in numerous studies (e.g., Eisner, 1970; Gough and Olton, 1972). In contrast with the process of perceptual analysis featured in embedded-figures types of tasks, tests of speed of closure require the synthesis of a perceptual-gestalt by providing organization to an incomplete figure. It seems reasonable to suppose that in closure-speed tests—at least those which use difficult problems of this type—restructuring ability is as much required as it is in tests of closure flexibility.

Functional fixity. The problems used by Duncker (1945) in his studies of this phenomenon provide particularly clear examples of restructuring tasks. As might be expected from the restructuring hypothesis, field-independent subjects do better on this kind of problem (Glucksberg, 1956).

Conservation. The problems used by Piaget and Inhelder (1962) in their studies of conservation of physical properties of objects provide equally clear examples of restructuring tasks, and here again, consistent with the restructuring hypothesis, field-independent subjects have been found to do better (Grippin, Ohnmacht, and Clark, 1973; Pascual-Leone, 1969).

Representation of the horizontal coordinate. This kind of competence is measured by the well-known Piagetian water-level problem. Successful performance on this test, which has been related to RFT performance in a number of studies (e.g., Pascual-Leone, 1969; Willemsen, Buchholz, Budrow, and Geannacopulos, 1973), depends on overcoming the influence of the immediate visual field and so may be conceived to involve restructuring.

Perspectivism. The ability to recognize that another's perspective may be different from one's own and to adopt it if required has been called "perspectivism" by Werner (1948) and "decentration" by Piaget (Piaget and Inhelder, 1956). Spatial-visualization problems, which may be considered examples of perspectivism tasks, have been among the most widely studied in relation to field dependence-independence. In the typical spatial-visualization task the subject views a visual display and is required to imagine how the display would look if viewed from a position different from his own. It seems reasonable to suppose that cognitive restructuring is involved in the act of reorganizing the self-display field in order to experience that field from a different viewpoint. The extensive literature now on hand leaves no doubt that spatial-visualization ability is correlated with field independence (e.g., Gardner, Jackson, and Messick, 1960; Gough and Olton, 1972; McGilligan and Barclay, 1974).

In summary, the evidence suggests that field independence in perception of the upright is related to competence in restructuring a field in a variety of spatial-visual situations that present the subject with a stimulus configuration whose components are simultaneously present at different loci in the visual field.

Relation among Spatial Restructuring Dimensions

To examine the extent of self-consistency in cognitive-restructuring competence we turn now to studies of the interrelation among cognitive-restructuring dimensions themselves. In this section we consider studies that used spatial tasks, and in the next section studies that used both spatial and nonspatial tasks.

A number of studies have examined the relation between EFT performance and performance on tests of the various spatial restructuring dimensions considered in the previous section:[1] size constancy (e.g., Gardner, Jackson, and Messick, 1960; Perez, 1958); closure speed (e.g., Messick and French, 1975); functional fixity (Harris, cited in Witkin et al., 1962); conservation (e.g., Pascual-Leone, 1969); representation of the horizontal coordinate (Pascual-Leone, 1969); and perspectivism (e.g., Bergman and Engelbrektson, 1973; Gardner, Jackson, and Messick, 1960; Messick and French, 1975). With a high degree of consistency, these studies have found the positive relation to be expected for the hypothesis that people are self-consistent with regard to extent of competence in spatial restructuring.

Some of the studies on perspectivism deserve special men-

[1]Since most studies on this issue have been concerned with this particular relationship, we limit ourselves to these studies here.

tion because they implicate performance on tests important in the Piagetian enterprise. The three-mountain problem of Piaget and Inhelder has been considered to provide a good measure of perspectivism. In one of its common variants, the subject is shown a landscape model consisting of three mountains of different sizes and then shown pictures representing views of the model. Afterwards he is asked to place a doll in the positions it would have to take in order to see the landscape scenes shown in the pictures. Children who are more competent in the restructuring required on embedded-figures tests also do better in locating the doll correctly, as would be expected from the restructuring hypothesis (e.g., Finley, Solla, and Cowan, 1977; Okonji and Olagbaiye, 1975).

Performance on the EFT has also been related to performance on other kinds of spatial restructuring dimensions, not yet considered, providing further evidence of self-consistency in cognitive restructuring.

As one example, set-breaking has been studied with Einstellung problems. In one of the well-known examples of such a problem, the subject is required to obtain a specified quantity of water by appropriate manipulation of the contents of each of three jars of known capacity. The first few problems can be solved by one method only, the repetition of which induces a set. The set-inducing series is followed, first, by several "critical" problems that may be solved by the method used in the set-inducing problem or by a shorter method, and then by several "extinction" or set-breaking problems that may be solved by the shorter method only. For the set to be broken, the elements (jars) that have been used in a given pattern in the set-inducing series must be considered apart from that pattern and arranged into a new pattern. Ability to break the set on the extinction problem has been related to EFT performance in most studies (e.g., Busse, 1968; Guetzkow, 1951).

Also found to be related to performance on embedded-figures tests is manner of handling concept-attainment tasks. Studies of this relation have recently been reviewed elsewhere (Goodenough, 1976). The evidence indicates, in general, that people who are competent in spatial restructuring on an embedded-figures task tend to adopt an hypothesis-testing approach in visual discrimination learning (Nebelkopf and Dreyer, 1973). Such an approach signifies a participant role in learning. In contrast, people who do less well on the EFT tend to show what Woodworth (1938) early called a "composite photograph" style of learning, signifying a more passive role. Moreover, when directed to adopt an hypothesis-testing approach, such people respond to salient stimulus attributes rather than sampling broadly from the set of available stimulus attributes in constructing their hypotheses (e.g., Kirschenbaum, 1968; Shapson, 1973), as people with better EFT performance are likely to do.

Providing further evidence on the relation among spatial restructuring dimensions are the results of some factor-analytic studies. There is a consensus among factor analysts that closure flexibility, closure speed, and one or two spatial-visualization dimensions are separate first-order factors, and that these first-order factors are intercorrelated, belonging to a common second-order factor (e.g., Horn and Cattell, 1966; Pawlik, 1966; Royce, 1973; Vernon, 1972). This second-order factor has often been called a "visualization" dimension (e.g., Horn and Cattell, 1967; Royce, 1973). Horn and Cattell, for example, in their theory of fluid (GF) and crystallized (GC) intelligence, have defined visualization (GV) as a general nonintellectual factor, encompassing problems that require manipulation of figural material in the visual modality. Moreover, (GV) has sometimes been defined in the factor-analytic literature in terms very similar to those we have used in our definition of cognitive restructuring. For example, Horn (1965) offers the following interpretation of (GV):

> This involves the processes of imagining the way objects may change as they move in space, maintaining orientation with respect to objects in space, keeping configurations in mind, finding the Gestalt among disparate parts in a visual field and *maintaining a flexibility concerning other possible* structurings *of elements in space* [pp. 309–310, italics ours].

In summary, the evidence that has been reviewed is consistent with the hypothesis that people are self-consistent in extent of cognitive restructuring competence across spatial-visual tasks.[2]

Relation between Spatial and Nonspatial Restructuring Dimensions

We continue our examination of self-consistency in cognitive restructuring by considering whether it extends beyond the spatial types of situations considered thus far to tasks in the auditory and verbal domains.

A separate general auditory factor has been proposed in the theory of fluid and crystallized intelligence that is analogous to the visualization factor (e.g., Horn and Cattell, 1967), and there is some evidence consistent with this proposition. A number of attempts have been made to identify speed and flexibility of closure in audition, and to relate these abilities to the visual closure factors (e.g., Fleishman, Roberts, and Friedman, 1958; Horn, 1973; Karlin, 1942; White, 1954). Correlations between visual and auditory tests have been reported in some of these studies, suggesting that the restructuring dimension extends beyond the purely visual mode. However, most of the available factor-analytic literature suggests a clear separation between restructuring in the visual and auditory modalities. The evidence on this point is not yet conclusive, however. Factor-analytic studies that include a variety of carefully constructed auditory tests, as well as visual tests to represent as many restructuring abilities as possible, are clearly needed to settle this issue (Horn, 1973).

[2]A further question has been raised about the role of spatial-visualization abilities in field dependence-independence (Sherman, 1967). It has also been proposed by several writers (e.g., Maccoby and Jacklin, 1974; Sherman, 1971) that the sex differences commonly found in tests of field dependence-independence are attributable to sex differences in visualization. The discussion of the relationship between field independence and visualization is somewhat confusing because each of these terms has been applied to specific first-order factors and more general higher-order factors. At the first-order level, the evidence is clear that separate flexibility-of-closure and spatial-visualization factors can be identified in visual functioning. At higher-order levels, however, it is unclear at the present time whether there are separate visualization (in Cattell's sense) and restructuring (as defined in this paper) abilities, or whether these terms simply reflect alternative hypotheses about the nature of the same general factor. Resolution of this issue will help to clarify the relation between sex differences in field dependence-independence and in visualization.

In considering the scope of the restructuring dimension, we also need to ask whether it extends into the verbal domain. The meaning of a word gives it an organization that may serve to embed the individual letters within it; phrases and sentences may similarly provide embedding contexts for constituent words in ways that appear analogous to what is done with figural material in embedded-figures tests. Moreover, there appear to be individual differences in the ability to overcome the effects of structure in a variety of verbal forms. However, most factor-analytic studies in the literature suggest that restructuring abilities in the verbal and visual-perceptual domains are not related very highly, if at all (e.g., Messick and French, 1975; Mooney, 1954; Podell and Phillips, 1959).

Messick and French (1975) have conducted the most comprehensive study to date of the relationships among closure tests in figural and verbal media. Included in that study were a number of tests specifically designed to measure speed of closure and flexibility of closure in verbal materials as well as in standard spatial reference tests of these factors. First-order factors emerged for speed and flexibility of closure in both spatial and verbal materials. More important, the spatial closure factors fused to form a second-order factor, which was unrelated to another second-order factor on which the verbal-closure tests emerged.

In evaluating the factor-analytic studies bearing on the restructuring hypothesis, the question arises as to whether the verbal tasks they employed are really analogous to visual disembedding tasks. The typical verbal-disembedding test involves rather limited aspects of linguistic functioning that are uncommon in ordinary language use. Many verbal disembedding tests require the subject to focus particularly on individual letters if he is to succeed at the assigned task. For example, he may be required to find hidden words in a sentence by combining the last several letters of one word with the first few letters of the immediately following word, letters which together form a new word. The rules of English impose sequential restrictions on the ways in which the letters may be combined. Accordingly, it is important in dealing with such tasks to check possible sequences of letters that can form new meaningful words. The atomistic orientation involved in focusing on letters apart from words, and the manipulation of letters to form words, are important skills in performing such tasks. These features may be sources of individual differences not present in disembedding in the spatial-configurational domain, where individual units are equivalent and advance constraints on how they may be ordered are not involved. The expertise some people show in games such as Scrabble provides a good illustration. Moreover, such expertise may be acquired through appropriate practice with the material. It is indeed plausible, as Cattell (1963) and Vernon (1965), among others, have suggested, that the ability to manipulate verbal material is primarily a function of traditional educational experience.

An alternative approach to the study of restructuring in the verbal domain is provided by modern psycholinguistics. In its concern with language development, and with the encoding and decoding processes in language production and comprehension, that field provides opportunities to examine verbal functioning more probingly than do the approaches commonly represented in factor-analytic studies. Little work of this kind has been done as yet, but the results of the few studies on record are suggestive.

Linguistic ambiguity has received considerable attention in the psycholinguistic literature because of its recognized importance in both language use and language theory (Katz and Postal, 1964). Sentences are considered ambiguous when they are open to two or more semantic interpretations. Sentence disambiguating, which requires the subject to identify several meanings in an ambiguous sentence, meets the definition of a restructuring task, since the initially apprehended organization of the sentence must be changed to identify alternative interpretations.

Sentence ambiguity may occur at three levels: at a lexical level, when a word or phrase has different meanings; at a surface-structure level, when alternate groupings of phrases are possible; and at an underlying-structure level, when alternative logical relations exist at a deep level (e.g., Chomsky, 1965; Foss, Bever, and Silver, 1968; MacKay, 1966). Sentences in which the ambiguity is at deeper linguistic levels are more difficult to disambiguate than sentences in which the ambiguity is at a surface level (MacKay and Bever, 1967). In our terms, ambiguity of greater complexity provides a greater challenge to restructuring skill.

A relation between sentence disambiguation and EFT performance has been reported by Goodman (1971) and Lefever and Ehri (1976). Goodman, for example, presented her subjects with a set of ambiguous sentences, some of which were lexically ambiguous and others syntactically ambiguous at a surface- or deep-structure level. In one experimental condition, subjects were informed that each sentence could be interpreted in more than one way and were asked to describe all the meanings it contained. As Goodman had predicted, performance on an embedded-figures type of test was not significantly related to disambiguating ability with the lexically ambiguous sentences, where the need for restructuring skill is relatively limited. When presented with a challenging restructuring task in the form of syntactically ambiguous sentences, however, EFT scores related to disambiguating ability as expected. In a second experimental manipulation, the subjects were given a set of alternative interpretations of each ambiguous sentence, some correct and others incorrect; their task was to choose the correct ones. In this condition, the job of restructuring had in effect already been performed by the experimenter and the subject's task was limited to checking the validity of each option. Here, with the need for restructuring skill eliminated, no relation was found with EFT scores. The work on sentence disambiguation suggests that restructuring in deep linguistic processing is related to restructuring in the visual-perceptual domain.

A recent study by Powers and Lis (1977) on grammatical transformation leads to the same conclusion. In this study, children were presented with a series of statements either in the active or passive voice, followed by questions in either the active or passive voice. Some of the statement-question combinations were in the same voice, so that no transformation was required; others were in the opposite voice, thus requiring transformation of the statement for the question to be answered. Alternative answers to each question were given and the child was required to choose the correct one. Children with limited competence on the EFT did significantly poorer on items requiring transformation than on items which did not. In contrast, children who did well on the EFT were no different on the two kinds of items. Since grammatical transformation would seem to involve cognitive restructuring in the verbal domain, these results also suggest self-consistency in cognitive restructuring ability across spatial and verbal functioning.

The work on sentence disambiguation and grammatical transformation points to the value of using tests of restructuring at deeper psycholinguistic levels in further studies of the generality of restructuring competence.

In summary, there is some evidence for a general cognitive restructuring dimension, although the hypothesis that the dimension may be limited to spatial-visual material cannot be rejected on the basis of the evidence now on hand.

The Nature of Field Dependence-Independence in Perception of the Upright

As we have seen, in the history of our work the field-dependence-independence dimension was first defined as reliance on gravitational-vs.-visual cues in perception of the upright. Subsequently, performance on tests of perception of the upright was reinterpreted as a perceptual disembedding ability. Both these hypotheses about the nature of individual differences in perception of the upright can now be more sharply defined and need to be reexamined on the basis of more recent evidence.

The first (gravitational-vs.-visual) hypothesis suggests that individual differences in the immediate perception of tilt in the RFT and BAT are a function of some kind of weighted average of sensory inputs from gravitational and visual receptors. In this view, field-independent people function with a greater degree of autonomy from the external visual field. Recent evidence suggests that visual and vestibular inputs summate at the level of the vestibular nucleus to produce perception of body motion (e.g., Henn, Young, and Finley, 1974), and it seems reasonable to assume a similar summation for the immediate perception of body orientation (e.g., Dichgans, Held, Young, and Brandt, 1972). We may thus suppose that extent of field dependence-independence in the BAT is determined by the relative weights assigned, perhaps at a subcortical level, to inputs from the vestibular otolith organ, varying with actual body position, and from the visual system, varying with extent of displacement of the visual field.

For the RFT there is experimental evidence to suggest that rod adjustments to the apparent visual vertical may be determined by a combination of a visually induced ocular rotation (torsion) in the direction of the tilted visual frame (Goodenough, Sigman, Oltman, Rosso, and Mertz, 1979; Greenberg, 1960; Hughes, 1973), and a visually induced illusion of self-tilt in the opposite direction (Ebenholtz and Benzschawel, 1977; Sigman, Goodenough, and Flannagan, 1978; Sigman, Goodenough, and Flannagan, 1979); both effects may be due to visual driving of the vestibular system.

Several studies have also reported RFT performance by supine observers viewing an overhead rod-and-frame display. The gravitational direction is irrelevant to the task in the supine position, but the subject may be asked to align the rod with the longitudinal body axis (Brosgole and Cristal, 1967; Lichtenstein and Saucer, 1974; Templeton, 1973). These studies have found that the effect of the tilted visual field is greater in the supine than in the erect position. The increased error in the supine RFT suggests that gravitational cues are helpful in the erect RFT. Thus, it is possible to suppose that individual differences in the standard RFT are a function of the relative weights assigned to vestibular and visual information.

With regard to the second (disembedding) hypothesis, we now consider disembedding to be an act of cognitive restructuring. To interpret BAT or RFT performance in terms of restructuring ability would require the assumption that the observer's immediate perception of tilt can be restructured to meet the task requirement of adjusting the rod or body to the gravitational upright. Although it seems unlikely that vestibular and visual inputs to the feeling of self-tilt can be separated perceptually, tactile-kinesthetic sensations may provide valid, distinctive cues to the gravitational upright that may be used by people with high restructuring ability to correct the primary perception of tilt. In this view the field-independent observer has an immediate, visually-induced illusion of tilt on the BAT and RFT, but is able to restructure this percept to meet the task requirement by reference to tactile-kinesthetic sensations.

If disembedding ability is indeed responsible for individual differences in perception of the upright, then in factor analyses the BAT and RFT should emerge on the same factor as the EFT, which characteristically loads a flexibility-of-closure factor. The evidence on this point is not yet clear, however. It is apparent that tests of perception of the upright belong in the same factor domain as tests of closure flexibility, closure speed, and spatial visualization. Almost invariably, the RFT and BAT have loaded one or more of the same factors as other tests in this cluster. However, there has not yet been a study with enough reference tests to determine the precise location of tests of perception of the upright within the cluster.

To our knowledge, there are only two factor-analytic studies that have used more than a single test to assess field dependence-independence in perception of the upright (Goodenough and Karp, 1961; Karp, 1963). In both studies a factor emerged loading all measures of perception of the upright, as well as tests of the other restructuring dimensions included in the test battery. However, neither study used enough reference tests for closure flexibility, closure speed, and spatial-visualization to permit these factors to emerge as separate. Other studies, which used the RFT, along with markers for other factors in the cluster, have usually found the RFT on the same factor as tests of closure flexibility, and occasionally closure speed and spatial visualization as well, but these studies did not have enough reference tests of perception of the upright (e.g., Bergman and Engelbrektson, 1973; Eisner, 1970; McWhinnie, 1970a; Pascual-Leone, 1969; Vernon, 1972). Because of these limitations in the factor-analytic studies on record, it is not clear in the present state of the evidence whether the RFT and BAT belong on the closure-flexibility factor or whether there exists a distinct factor involving reliance on vestibular-vs.-visual sources of information.

There is some evidence from experimental and correlational studies, and from observations made under altered gravitational conditions, which suggests that a vestibular-vs.-visual

factor may be involved in tests of perception of the upright. People who are field dependent on the RFT have been found more susceptible to a variety of illusions of self-movement that are induced by movement of the visual field (e.g., Barrett, Thornton, and Cabe, 1970; Nilsson, Magnusson, and Vasko, 1972). For example, Nilsson et al. report that their field-dependent subjects showed larger illusory shifts of the median plane when viewing a visual field that is rotating around them. The work of Nilsson et al. is particularly interesting because it also suggests that field-independent people may be more susceptible than field-dependent people to visual illusions induced by self-rotation. Their field-independent subjects showed a greater oculogyral illusion, in which a visual stimulus located directly in front of and revolving with the rotating subject appears to move laterally. The oculogyral illusion is sometimes used as a measure of semicircular-canal sensitivity (Graybiel, Kerr, and Bartley, 1948). These results are difficult to account for on the basis of the disembedding hypothesis. They suggest rather that RFT performance may tap a dimension of functioning in which what is at issue is the relative weights assigned to vestibular-vs.-visual sources of information. They also suggest that the dimension is bipolar, in the sense that, while field-dependent people are particularly susceptible to illusions induced by displacement of the visual field, field-independent people may be particularly susceptible to other illusions induced by vestibular stimulation.

Another source of evidence on the nature of individual differences in perception of the upright that seems consistent with the vestibular-vs.-visual hypothesis comes from reports of the experiences of the astronauts who participated in the Skylab space program. In the Skylab environment, many of the astronauts felt uncomfortable and apparently experienced feelings of self-tilt when their bodies were out of alignment with the visual verticals of their cabin. Moreover, reports of the astronauts' experiences clearly indicate that there were dramatic individual differences in the visually-induced feelings of self-tilt (Cooper, 1976a, 1976b). One of the astronauts, at least, was relatively unaffected by the visual axes of space. For him, the vertical axis was defined egocentrically: "'. . . up is over your head, down is below your feet'" (1976a, p. 40). Under zero-G conditions there is no possibility that individual differences in perception of self-tilt could be due to disembedding ability in the use of tactile-kinesthetic cues.[3] The fact that dramatic individual differences occur in the supine RFT, where gravitationally-induced, tactile-kinesthetic cues to the egocentric vertical are also absent, should be noted here as well (e.g., Lichtenstein and Saucer, 1974). It would be particularly interesting to know whether the supine RFT is related to tests of restructuring ability, as is the erect RFT. If it is, then this relationship would also be difficult to understand in terms of disembedding ability in the use of tactile kinesthetic cues in the RFT.

In summary, while more experimental research is needed on the specific processes involved in RFT and BAT performance, the available evidence appears to favor the view that individual differences in perception of the upright may be due to a bipolar dimension of reliance on vestibular-vs.-visual cues, and that this dimension is distinguishable from, though related to, the unipolar dimensions of restructuring ability.

The New Evidence: Social Behavior

Autonomy in Interpersonal Relations

An extensive body of research on interpersonal behavior has shown that people who are field independent in perception of the upright function more autonomously of others than do field-dependent people. The tendencies to rely primarily on internal or external referents that individuals show in perception of the upright thus appear to have a direct counterpart in their behavior in the interpersonal domain. The evidence on this relation has recently been reviewed elsewhere (Witkin and Goodenough, 1977), so we only summarize it here.

[3]In view of the evidence that pilots (e.g., Cullen, Harper, and Kidera, 1969) and engineers (e.g., Barrett and Thornton, 1967) tend to be field independent, we assume that, in standard tests of perception of the upright, the astronauts are likely to be relatively field independent as well. However, individual differences among relatively field-independent subjects might still be expected under the more challenging conditions of space.

A number of studies of interacting social groups have shown that, under conditions where the information available to them is unclear or inadequate, people who rely on the external visual field in perception of the upright make greater use of information from others in arriving at their own views than do people who tend to rely on the body (e.g., Antler, 1964; Balance, 1967; Birmingham, 1974; Busch and DeRidder, 1973; Linton, 1955; Nordquist, 1958; Shaffer, 1970; Shulman, 1975; Solar, Davenport, and Bruehl, 1969; Wachman, 1964; Weinberg, 1970). However, studies that used unambiguous tasks have found little relation between RFT scores and response to external social referents (e.g., Krippner and Brown, 1973; Morgan, 1972; Roberts, 1964). Moreover, other important aspects of dependence beyond information seeking (such as emotional attachment to others, responsiveness to extrinsic social rewards, cooperativeness, and approval seeking) appear to bear little relation to field dependence in perception of the upright (e.g., Dolson, 1973; Eberhard and Nilsson, 1967; Gillies and Bauer, 1971; Gordon, 1954; Kagan, Zahn, and Gealy 1977; Lopez, 1976; McCarrey, 1969; Morelan and Ortiz, 1975; Paclisanu, 1970; Throckmorton, 1974; Webb, 1972; Weissman, 1971).

The pattern of results found with tests of perception of the upright has also been observed in most studies that used the EFT (e.g., Adler, Gervasi, and Holzer, 1973; Beckerle, 1966; Brandsma, 1971; Cooperman, 1976; Crutchfield, 1957; DeWitt and Averill, 1976; Doebler, 1977; Farley, 1974; Hoffman, 1975; Irwin, Klein, Engle, Yarbrough, and Nerlove, 1977; Klebanoff, 1975; Paeth, 1973; Palmer and Field, 1971; Raab, 1973; Rohde, 1977; Rosner, 1956; Soat, 1974; Swan, 1973). People who are better at disembedding are less likely to have recourse to external sources of information when dealing with ambiguous social tasks.

Further evidence that people who are field independent in perception of the upright also function more autonomously in their interpersonal relations comes from the repeated characterization of them by others as being high in autonomy and as showing initiative, responsibility-taking, self-reliance, and the ability to think for themselves; similar relations with personal characteristics have also been found with the EFT (Witkin and Goodenough, 1977).

Still another kind of evidence bearing on the autonomy issue comes from studies on self-object differentiation, all carried out within the framework of Mahler's separation-individuation model (Mahler, 1966; Mahler, Pine, and Bergman, 1975). Three of these studies compared young children's standing on the separation-individuation dimension with their performance on an EFT task. Paul (1975) inferred degree of separation-individuation in her young subjects from the extent of difficulty they experienced in separating from their parents after one week of nursery school. Children who gave evidence of less difficulty in separation were relatively better at disembedding. A similar relation was found by Olesker (1978) when she assessed self-object differentiation through extended observation of a small group of young children in a nursery school setting. Baraga (1977) observed that more attachment behavior at age one was associated with less competence in disembedding at age three (Baraga, 1977).

Winestine (1969), in a more extensive and complex investigation, which used twins as subjects, confirmed and extended these findings. A twin is not only confronted with the usual developmental task of individuating himself from his mother, but he faces the additional and perhaps equally difficult task of individuating himself from his twin. Moreover, the mother, in dealing with a twinship, has the option of treating it as a unit or as composed of two distinct beings. While these options exist in a mother's relationship with her non-twin children as well, the probability is greater that twins will be dealt with as a unit because they appear on the scene at the same time and grow up together. Since the separation-individuation issue takes so sharp a form in the twinship, Winestine saw the twinship as providing a particularly good opportunity to examine the relationship between self-object differentiation and field dependence-independence. Winestine's expectation was, of course, that twins who had made greater progress toward individuation would be more field independent.

In the study Winestine did, the extent of that progress was inferred from the strength of the twinning reaction of each member of 30 pairs of male twins described by their parents as identical. Assessments of the strength of the reaction were based on evidence from an interview with each boy; the twinning reaction was judged to be stronger the greater the inter-identification of the boy with his co-twin. As predicted, boys rated as showing a stronger twinning reaction earned significantly lower index scores, based on a composite of measures from the RFT, BAT, and EFT, indicating that they were more field dependent and less competent at disembedding.

Still further evidence on autonomy comes from a research route quite different from those considered thus far: studies of the degree to which patients in psychotherapy give evidence of wanting or needing the theapist to provide structure for them, suggesting less autonomous functioning.

In one study (Koff, 1972), patients' expectancies were examined prior to therapy, using for this purpose the Berzins Psychotherapy Expectancy Inventory and the Williams Expectancy Inventory. Patients who did less well on an EFT task responded significantly more often in the affirmative to a cluster of items on the Berzins instrument that reflected the expectation that the therapist would provide them with advice and guidance. They also responded more positively to a cluster of Williams' items defined as involving "the expectancy of interacting in a structure-seeking or criticism anticipating manner (patient role) with a knowledgeable, analytical, logical or evaluative 'expert' (therapist role)" (p. 28).[4]

These differences in need for structure, expressed prior to therapy, have been observed during therapy as well. In one study (Russakoff, Fontana, Dowds, and Harris, 1976) patients, after the first session of therapy, filled out a questionnaire concerned with the feelings and ease of communication between themselves and their therapists. Patients who were more field dependent on the RFT scored higher on a scale derived from questionnaire responses that reflected degree of dissatisfaction with lack of structure during the session. Consistent with the patients' own reactions, therapists checked as applying significantly more often to their field-dependent than their field-independent patients the questionnaire item: "The patient wanted me to tell him what to talk about." Another study (Dowds,

[4]These patterns were not found when the therapy expectancy instruments were administered to a group of college students, but it is difficult to see how these questionnaires were relevant for people not going into therapy.

Fontana, Russakoff, and Harris, 1977), using the same therapist item for patients who had received the RFT, confirmed these results.

Similar in outcome is a study by Greene (1979) which showed that participants in a group dynamics training conference (patterned after the Tavistock Institute of Human Relations model) who did less well on the EFT reacted more negatively to a large, less structured group context and more positively to a small group setting, as compared to participants who did well on the EFT. However, a study by Rappoport (1975) with human potential groups of high and low structure did not find the expected relation between participants' reactions to degree of structure and EFT performance. A final study (Austrian, 1976) used a "therapy analogue situation," consisting of a structured-interview component and a free-association ambiguous component. College students who were relatively field dependent on the RFT and did less well on the EFT described themselves, on self-report scales, as less comfortable in the unstructured situation; and they showed a larger difference in affect between the structured and ambiguous conditions. Moreover, judges rated them as less productive in the ambiguous condition, thus showing that not only feelings but effectiveness of performance as well were adversely affected when these subjects found themselves in an ambiguous situation. This observation is consistent with the results of several studies (e.g., deGroot, 1968; Freedman, O'Hanlon, Oltman, and Witkin, 1972; Steingart, Freedman, Grand, and Buchwald, 1975) with the Gottschalk and Gleser (1969) five-minute monologue association method that requires the subject to speak while the experimenter just listens.

These differences in need for structure by patients in therapy appear to be easily "read" by therapists early in their encounters with patients. This is shown by an analysis (described in Witkin, Moore, Goodenough, and Cox, 1977) of therapy transcripts from a study by Witkin, Lewis, and Weil (1968). Therapists in that study asked significantly more open-ended questions of patients who were field independent on the RFT and BAT and who did well on the EFT; they asked more questions of a specific nature, allowing "yes" or "no" answers, of patients who were at the opposite extreme of these tests. In the first kind of question the therapist leaves it to the patient to structure his answer on his own, whereas the second kind of question serves to help the patient compose the information that the therapist is seeking. While the Witkin, Lewis, and Weil study did not examine outcome effects, it seems plausible that the use of open-ended questions may be troublesome to the patient who experiences difficulty in structuring; and the use of specific questions may be troublesome to the patient who feels able to do his own structuring. An inappropriate questioning mode may well have an adverse effect on the patient's relationship with the therapist, so that by adapting his questions to the patient's needs the therapist may be contributing to a better therapeutic outcome.

Further evidence that therapists recognize patients' need for help in structuring, or their ability to function autonomously, comes from studies of treatment modalities recommended for different kinds of patients. Studies by Greene (1972) and by Karp, Kissin, and Hustmeyer (1970) both showed that therapists favored supportive forms of therapy for patients who did less well on the EFT and modifying forms for patients who did relatively well.

The evidence reviewed in this section, much of it drawn from real-life situations, shows rather impressively that people who function more autonomously of the external visual field in perception of the upright also function more autonomously of others in interpersonal relations. Equally well supported is the relation between interpersonal autonomy and performance in restructuring tasks such as the EFT.

Interpersonal Competencies

Another kind of evidence from the recent research on social behavior has shown that people who are field dependent in perception of the upright and limited in disembedding ability have an interpersonal orientation, whereas people who are field independent and competent in disembedding have an impersonal orientation. Thus, the former kinds of people, more than the latter, pay selective attention to social cues; they favor situations that bring them into contact with others over solitary situations; they prefer educational-vocational domains that are social in content and require working with people; they seek physical closeness to people in their social interactions; and they are more open in their feelings (see Witkin and Goodenough, 1977, for a recent review).

These attributes of an interpersonal orientation are likely to put people who show them in good touch with what others may be thinking and feeling. Such an outcome may indeed be adaptive for field-dependent people by giving them ready access to information that may help them structure ambiguous situations, something they are not easily able to do on their own. It is also reasonable to hypothesize that these attributes, compared to those constituting an impersonal orientation, make for more extended experience with people and greater opportunity to build up a fund of knowledge and techniques for dealing with others, thereby contributing to facility in getting along with people. Other characteristics that have been ascribed to people who are field dependent on tests of perception of the upright and who do less well on the EFT have similar implications. These characteristics include warm, affectionate, tactful, accommodating, nonevaluative and accepting of others, not likely to express hostility directly against others when such feelings are aroused in an interpersonal context. They contrast with those reported for people who are field independent and do well on the EFT: demanding, inconsiderate, manipulating others as a means of achieving personal ends, cold and distant in relations with others (Witkin and Goodenough, 1977).

While there is considerable evidence that field-dependent people, compared to field-independent ones, show more of the social behaviors, attributes, and habitual ways of reacting likely to contribute to facility in getting along with others, studies in which competence in social-interpersonal situations has been directly assessed have only recently begun to appear in the literature (see Witkin and Goodenough, 1977). The results thus far appear consistent with expectations. For example, one study found that students judged to be competent in psychiatric nursing were relatively field dependent on the RFT, whereas those judged competent in surgical nursing were relatively field independent (Quinlan and Blatt, 1972). Obviously, effectiveness in

the role of nurse with psychiatric patients rests heavily on competence in interpersonal relations; effectiveness in surgical nursing does not, depending rather on cognitive restructuring skills. Similar in implication are the findings of a study by MacKinnon (1962) that showed that writers judged to be outstanding by their peers did relatively less well on the EFT, compared to architects, who did well. Many writing forms depend for their effectiveness on accurate portrayal of people and of interpersonal relations. That competence is not important in architecture where cognitive restructuring skills are clearly essential to effective performance. It has also been found that groups with field-dependent members tend to be relatively more effective in conflict resolution than groups without them (Oltman, Goodenough, Witkin, Freedman, and Friedman, 1975; Shulman, 1975). Such people thus make a greater contribution to the effectiveness of group functioning, as judged by the criterion of achievement of a consensus.

To summarize what we have said about them, people who are field dependent in perception of the upright and competent at disembedding, have more extended experience with others, which in turn is likely to foster the acquisition of information about people and ways of interacting with them. Such people also show more of the social behaviors and attributes important for effective interpersonal relations, and there is some beginning evidence that they may be better able to get along with others. These features, in the collective, constitute interpersonal competencies.

We know very little as yet about the social skills of field-independent people, beyond the evidence that they are limited in interpersonal competencies. We may speculate, however, that their social skills are likely to represent the application of their restructuring skills to the social domain, rather than investment in relations with others.

One of the ways in which restructuring may show itself in the social domain is in the organizing and ordering of social situations. Thus, in their interest-inventory responses, people who do well on the EFT have been found to favor production management in contrast to the preference for personnel management among people who do less well (e.g., Clar, 1971; Pierson,

1965). Similarly, therapists who were field independent on the RFT have been found to favor a highly directive or non-involving role in therapy (Pollack and Kiev, 1963); and teachers who were competent at disembedding favored the use of a lecture or discussion approach in teaching, both of which leave to the teacher a large role in directing student learning (Wu, 1967).

Another way in which field-independent people may show their restructuring ability in the social domain is in their apparently greater social perspectivism. Thus, people who do relatively well on the EFT have been found to show greater perspectivism on Feffer's (1959) egocentrism task (e.g., Fiscalini, 1974; Futterer, 1973; Perkins, 1973). This evidence must be treated with caution, however, since the task used was of a verbal-hypothetical nature, raising the possibility that it was handled essentially as a cognitive problem, so that its results may not generalize to behavior in interpersonal situations. Still another way in which people who are field independent in perception of the upright may show restructuring competence in the social domain is in the greater accuracy they have been reported to show in person perception (e.g., Cooper, 1967; Wolitzky, 1973). Here again caution is indicated since the studies involved used highly cognitive tasks that encouraged an analytical, problem-solving orientation, so that judgments made may have reflected cognitive restructuring ability more than accuracy in person perception.[5] These various hints that

[5]Consistent with this possibility are the results of a recent study in our laboratory by Rapaczynski, Welkowitz, and Sadd (1979) on judgment of affect. Subjects in that study listened to 15-minute segments of tapes of therapy sessions and were then required to judge the extent of warmth felt by the therapist toward the patient and the patient toward the therapist. Comparing these judgments with the actual ratings made by therapist and patient on their felt warmth toward each other during the session, subjects who did less well on the EFT proved to be significantly more accurate in their judgments. The 15-minute listening sessions allowed prolonged immersion in an engrossing emotional situation, thereby fostering a participant type of experience. This and other features of the situation worked against development of the problem-solving, analytical approach emphasized in the Cooper and Wolitzky studies. Finally, the affect to be judged—warmth—is one that is probably best estimated through immediate global apprehension. This constellation of task features seems likely to favor the makeup of people who are field dependent and limited in restructuring ability, thereby accounting for their better performance in the Rapaczynski, Welkowitz, and Sadd study.

the social skills of field-independent people may be primarily expressions of their restructuring ability are hardly conclusive, but they suggest areas of study in the much needed research on the social skills such people may have.

Reflecting the relatively late entry of the social domain in the development of research on field dependence-independence, our knowledge of the social skills associated with that dimension is still limited. Further delineation of the interpersonal competencies particular to more field-dependent people and identification of the social skills to be found among field-independent people are important research tasks that lie ahead.

Proposals for Theory Revision

The evidence that has been reviewed points to the need to reconsider our earlier conception of field dependence-independence and indicates some directions that theory revision and extension may profitably take. We now outline the main theoretical changes that seem plausible on the basis of the newer evidence and suggest ways of further testing the conceptual model that has emerged through these changes.

Distinctiveness of Cognitive Restructuring and Reliance on Vestibular-vs.-Visual Referents

It now seems possible that what we earlier designated an articulated-global field approach consists of two separate though related functions: reliance on vestibular or visual-field referents and cognitive restructuring. In this conception we revert to our very earliest view of performance on tests of perception of the upright, and put in question our subsequently held view that at the essence of performance in both tests of perception of the upright and tests such as the EFT is competence in disembedding.

Autonomy of External Referents in Perceptual and Social Behavior

Another proposal for theory revision emerges from the newer evidence of studies stimulated by the concept of articulated-global cognitive functioning combined with the newer evidence on interpersonal behavior. As we have seen, numerous studies of interacting social groups have made it quite clear that people who maintain their autonomy of the external visual field in perception of the upright are also likely to function more autonomously of external social frames of reference in their interpersonal relations, particularly under conditions of ambiguity. The tendencies to rely on external sources of information under ambiguous conditions, or to function more independently of such information, manifest themselves whether the source is other people with whom the person is interacting or the visual field in perception of the upright. In this new view, the individual differences that have been observed in performance on tests of perception of the upright and in interpersonal relations have a common basis: both reflect degree of autonomy of external referents or extent of reliance on self.[6]

This pattern of relations between cognitive and social behaviors is similar to that observed in the factor analytic work of Cattell and his colleagues on dimensions of temperament in objective tests (e.g., Cattell, 1955, 1957; Cattell and Warburton, 1967; Hundleby, Pawlik, and Cattell, 1965). Although Cattell has not used tests of perception of the upright, this work

[6]The field-dependence-independence construct is conceptually quite different from other constructs to which they bear a surface similarity. One of these is locus of control. Numerous studies have shown that, with rare exceptions, measures of the two dimensions are unrelated (e.g., Roodin, Broughton, and Vaught, 1974; Shapson, 1973; Tobacyk, Broughton, and Vaught, 1975). Whereas field dependence-independence is a process variable, representing degree of autonomous functioning in assimilating information from self and field, locus of control is an attitudinal or belief variable, representing expectancies of internal or external control of reinforcement, or greater or less fatalism as an outlook toward life. Field dependence-independence is also distinctly different from extraversion-introversion. Numerous studies, again with few exceptions, have not found any relation between measures of the two dimensions (e.g., Cegalis and Leen, 1977; DuPreez, 1967; Lester, 1976). Finally, another cognitive style, reflection-impulsivity, assessed by the MFFT, has been found to show a modest relation with field dependence-independence (Messer, 1976), although the basis of the relation is not entirely clear. While the less structured controls of relatively field-dependent people (Witkin, Goodenough, and Oltman, 1979) may play a role in their more rapid ("impulsive") responses on the MFFT, it is also possible that differences in the concept-attainment strategies characteristically used by field-dependent and field-independent people (Goodenough, 1976) may contribute to differences in MFFT performance.

is particularly relevant because at least one measure of closure speed and one of closure flexibility, both of which we consider cognitive-restructuring dimensions, have been included from the earliest study in the series (Cattell, 1948), and have defined a temperament factor called U.I.19. As in the evolution of our own work, Cattell's concept of the personality correlates of speed and flexibility of closure has periodically been revised to fit newly-available data. Viewed in historical perspective, our conception of the field-dependence-independence dimension and Cattell's conception of U.I.19 in fact appear to be converging. U.I.19 was early interpreted as an accuracy factor called "Critical Exactness" or "Critical Practicality" (Cattell, 1957). As the network of evidence on personality characteristics expanded, however, the interpretive emphasis appropriately shifted. This shift is reflected in changes in title to "Promethean Will vs. Subduedness" (Hundleby, Pawlik, and Cattell, 1965) and more recently to "Independence vs. Subduedness" (Cattell and Warburton, 1967). While some differences remain between Cattell's interpretation of his independence factor and our conception of field independence, it seems obvious to us, as well as to Cattell (1969) and Royce (1973), that there is an important area of overlap between the work of U.I.19 and on field independence.

INTERRELATIONS AMONG AUTONOMY, COGNITIVE RESTRUCTURING SKILLS, AND INTERPERSONAL COMPETENCIES

It appears that greater individual autonomy is associated with competence in cognitive restructuring, while greater reliance on external referents is associated with a set of interpersonal competencies. The evidence that has recently become available suggests a model in which these variables are hierarchically ordered, with autonomous functioning, in both perception of the upright and in interpersonal behavior, at the apex of the cluster, as a broad superordinate construct, and cognitive restructuring skills and interpersonal competencies as subsidiary constructs, at a level below the apex. At the next lower level are to be found specific cognitive-restructuring and interpersonal-competence variables. This proposal carries no necessary implications as to the effects the three main components of the model—autonomy, cognitive restructuring, and interpersonal competence—exert upon one another to produce the pattern we find among them, but some causal connections may be suggested.

We are first of all inclined to regard the development of interpersonal competencies as the outcome of limited self-nonself segregation and, with it, limited autonomy. The interpersonal orientation of people who are field dependent in perception of the upright and the impersonal orientation of field-independent people may be conceived as adaptations to their tendencies to function in more autonomous or less autonomous fashion. The constituents of the interpersonal orientation of field-dependent people are in effect a repertoire of behaviors that give them access to external referents when they are needed. These behaviors are not as evident in field-independent people who, relying more on the self, have less need for them. The greater involvement of field-dependent people with others, in its turn, is likely to facilitate the formation of norms and behavior expectancies for different kinds of people, in a variety of social circumstances, and the acquisition of experience in dealing with others. The experience of field-dependent people in social interaction, in combination with their social characteristics, may reasonably be expected to contribute to effectiveness in getting along with others. Field-independent people, on the other hand, with their greater self-nonself segregation, are capable of structuring situations on their own. Because they are able to function with greater autonomy, they show greater polarity between self and others and are not as likely to develop the social characteristics or to have the extended experience in social interaction that foster the development of interpersonal competencies. The interpersonal competencies involved in getting along with others found among field-dependent people, we are suggesting, are the sequelae of the tendency to rely on external referents.

We turn next to the relation that has been established between cognitive restructuring ability and the tendency to function autonomously of external referents. Within differentiation theory there are several ways of accounting for that relationship in causal terms.

Whether a person tends to rely primarily on external referents or to be self-reliant may influence development of his manner of processing information from the field—specifically, whether he will restructure the field on his own, or accede to its dominant properties. A person who functions less autonomously would appear likely to adhere to the field as given in dealing with cognitive restructuring tasks. A more autonomous person may be more likely "to go beyond the information given," when this is required by situational demands or inner needs. "Acting on the field" may take different forms. It may entail breaking up an organized field so that its parts are experienced as discrete from background; providing organization to a field that lacks it; or imposing a different organization on a field from the one suggested by its inherent organization. It is because such actions involve changing the field, rather than taking it "as is," that we have designated them acts of restructuring. In this new view, the development of cognitive restructuring skills is rooted in such basic characteristics as developed self-nonself segregation and individual autonomy. To the extent that cognitive restructuring skills have their origins in such basic characteristics of the person, these skills should show themselves pervasively in the behavior of the person to whom such referents are available. Though self-consistency is postulated, it may be moderated by unique effects of the particular sense modality (e.g., visual or auditory), medium (e.g., figural or symbolic), and processing (e.g., simultaneous or sequential) involved in any given cognitive restructuring task.

Differentiation theory suggests another way of conceptualizing the relationship between autonomous functioning and cognitive restructuring skills, which has been considered in detail elsewhere (Witkin, Goodenough, and Oltman, 1979). Reflecting the organismic character of differentiation, people who show greater psychological differentiation, as reflected in a field-independent mode of functioning, also give evidence of greater hemispheric differentiation (i.e., lateralization of the cerebral hemispheres). Levy (1969, 1974) has recently put forward a proposal about possible cognitive consequences of greater or less cerebral lateralization. That proposal suggests that when verbal and spatial functions are incompletely lateralized in the left and right hemispheres, verbal functions tend to predominate at the expense of spatial functions. Consequently, verbal functions may be carried out as effectively among field-dependent people, who tend to be less lateralized, as among field-independent people, who are more lateralized. On the other hand, spatial functions, and perhaps spatial-restructuring functions in particular, may not be performed as well by field-dependent people as they are by field-independent people. It would follow from this view that spatial restructuring abilities would be related to other aspects of differentiation, but verbal restructuring would not. As we have seen, the evidence on the relation between spatial and verbal restructuring is not yet definitive, however.

To whatever degree cognitive restructuring skills are direct expressions of individual differences in autonomy or are mediated by hemispheric lateralization, it seems reasonable to assign reliance on external referents-vs.-autonomous functioning the status of a higher-level construct. Major support for this is to be found in the large cross-cultural literature on field dependence-independence, recently reviewed by Witkin and Berry (1975) and examined in later sections of this monograph. That literature suggests that in societies which encourage autonomy from parental and social authority in children while they are growing up, we more commonly find people who show the cluster of field independence in perception of the upright, competence in cognitive restructuring, and self-reliance, as compared to people from societies that emphasize conformity. Greater or less autonomy is thus implicated as the centerpiece in the development of the characteristics we have found to be associated with each other.

It is clear that much additional work is needed to check the model we have here proposed. At the moment, evidence for the model is more extensive in regions concerned with perceptual and intellectual functioning—particularly those for which paper-and-pencil tests have been available so as to allow group testing—than it is in other regions; constructs concerned with interpersonal behavior have received relatively limited attention, as we have seen. As a result of this uneven development of the empirical underpinning, the details of the structure are clearer in some regions than in others.

Among the propositions of the model on which further evidence is needed are the distinctiveness of the functions involved in perception of the upright and cognitive restructuring; the generality of the restructuring dimension; and the hierarchical ordering of the constructs in the model. These propositions are all amenable to further check by a variety of approaches: experimental methods, factor analyses, and training procedures.

To illustrate, the issue of the distinctiveness of the processes involved in performance on tests of perception of the upright, such as the RFT and BAT, and on cognitive restructuring tasks, such as the EFT, lends itself to further inquiry by an experimental approach. That approach is illustrated by the studies cited earlier examining the role of specific bodily events in performance on the RFT, events that could hardly enter into performance of visual-spatial restructuring tasks such as the EFT. The processes involved in the RFT are not yet fully established, but, as we have seen, performance on this test is clearly amenable to experimental analysis to determine whether a visual-disembedding process is involved, or whether individual differences in perception of the upright are due entirely to factors such as visually-induced oculo-torsion and body-tilt effects. In addition to answering this question, an experimental analysis of RFT performance, and identification of its constituent processes, is likely to lead to separate measures of these processes that may be used in correlational studies of individual differences.

An appropriately designed factor-analytic study can provide an additional check on the distinctiveness of the functions involved in perception of the upright and cognitive restructuring. To be fruitful in assessing this issue, such a study, as we suggested earlier, would need to include a sufficient number of tests of both perception of the upright and of various cognitive restructuring dimensions to allow each to emerge as a separate factor, if they are indeed separate.

Sufficiently comprehensive, the kind of factor-analytic study proposed here can at the same time serve in the further assessment of the generality of cognitive restructuring ability. There is clear evidence of individual self-consistency in performance across spatial restructuring tests, but further evidence is needed on whether this self-consistency extends to auditory and verbal restructuring tasks as well. For adequate representation of the auditory domain, it is necessary to develop an array of tests that are the auditory counterparts of the tests used to assess the spatial restructuring dimensions. For proper representation of the verbal domain, tests need to be developed that, for reasons already considered, tap deeper levels of psycholinguistic functioning than do the verbal tests commonly used in factor analytic studies. We noted earlier that such features of particular cognitive restructuring tasks as sense modality, medium, and nature of processing involved may each make unique contributions to test performance above and beyond that made by cognitive restructuring per se. The evidence from the proposed study is likely to shed light on the role of such moderating factors.

Checks on the hierarchical ordering suggested by our model may be provided by a factor-analytic study that yields a pattern of relations among factor scores for the three major constructs: reliance on internal-vs.-external referents, cognitive restructuring skills, and interpersonal competencies. To achieve this purpose, the very considerable task must first be met of conceptualizing more precisely the nature of interpersonal competencies and devising tests for their assessment. As one check on the proposed hierarchical ordering, we may expect that if, as suggested, cognitive restructuring skills and interpersonal competencies are derivations of reliance on internal or external referents, measures of the internal-external dimension should relate more highly to measures of the cognitive and interpersonal variables than would the cognitive and interpersonal measures relate to each other. A factor-analytic study could also provide a check on the proposed hierarchical relation among reliance on internal-vs.-external referents, interpersonal competencies, and cognitive restructuring. If individual differences in reliance on self or field is a dimension located near the apex of the hierarchical structure, as we conceive it to be, not only would tests of perception of the upright define a separate factor from the cognitive restructuring factor lower down in the pyramid, but partialling out scores for a perception-of-the-upright factor should eliminate the correlations between measures of restructuring skills and interpersonal competencies.

Another possible approach to checking the hierarchical ordering proposed in our model is through the use of training procedures. If there is a general restructuring dimension, as our model suggests, we may expect a program of training in restructuring to affect performance on tests of each of the lower-order variables in which restructuring is considered to be involved: disembedding, perspectivism, verbal disambiguation, etc. To the extent that each lower-order variable involves cognitive restructuring, in addition to a specific component unique to that variable, training in restructuring should have a direct and immediate effect upon performance on tests of these variables. Whereas the hierarchical ordering we have proposed leads to the expectation that training in restructuring would result in improved performance on the lower-order dimensions in which it is involved, that proposal at the same time leads us to expect that training in restructuring may not have much effect on performance of tests of perception of the upright.

The value of a training approach in assessing the hierarchical character of our model may be illustrated by another kind of study using the psychotherapy situation, which in a very real sense involves training. In psychotherapy, a goal for many patients is achievement of greater personal autonomy. Success in that goal would, according to our model, contribute to increased skill in cognitive restructuring, even though therapy does not concern itself directly with betterment in that domain. In this instance, the consequences of training in autonomy upon the cognitive restructuring dimensions immediately below, are not likely to take as direct and immediate a form as training in cognitive restructuring is expected to have on its lower-order individual cognitive-restructuring dimensions. As internal referents are developed through therapy, they help provide the mediators necessary for acting on cognitive fields, or restructuring them. However, the specific mediators relevant to dealing with cognitive tasks need to be formed, and experience must be gained in their use. In a sense, training in autonomy may open opportunities for individual development more commonly available in earlier periods of life. Achievement of greater personal autonomy in a patient who, at the outset, is relatively reliant on external referents need not of course lead to the loss of the interpersonal competencies such a person is likely to have acquired through his earlier tendency to rely primarily on external referents. As is not uncommon in development, characteristics that are the products of developmental forces operative at one stage of growth may become enduring attributes of the person and may continue to express themselves, even though the forces which originally generated them are no longer operative.

In general, the model we have proposed not only provides a plausible way of conceptualizing the evidence now on hand, but, at least as important, it is amenable to further testing. Inevitably, the results of that testing may be expected to contribute to the further evolution of the model.

FIELD DEPENDENCE-INDEPENDENCE AS A COGNITIVE STYLE

The model presented has implications for both the conception of cognitive styles and for use of the designation field dependence-independence.

Over the long history of research on psychological differentiation, there have been continuous changes in the empirical picture and accompanying changes in nomenclature and conceptualization. "Field dependence-independence" and "cognitive style" were used, at different times, as labels for different dimensions in a hierarchical set. These variations, and particularly some of the more recent usages that have come into vogue, have created problems that have been the source of critical commentaries in the literature. We believe the model now proposed does not involve these problems and provides a conception of cognitive style more consistent with common usage than our previous conception.

The first problem the new conception addresses has arisen from the use of the term "field dependence-independence" in several different ways in the literature. Our very earliest use of the term, as we have seen, was for the dimension of individual differences in tendency to rely primarily on the visual field or the body as referents for perception of the upright. Later, it was used to refer to ability to overcome an embedding context in perception. Further studies of the scope of these individual differences showed them to be part of a still broader dimension, involving both analysis and structuring, in intellectual and perceptual activities. This broader dimension was designated an articulated-vs.-global field approach and was also conceived as an ability.

When we began to use the concept of cognitive style (e.g., Witkin, 1964, 1965; Witkin, Goodenough, and Karp, 1967), we applied it specifically to the articulated-global field-approach dimension. In using this concept we meant to emphasize several characteristics of the dimension. First, it is a pervasive dimension of individual functioning, showing itself in the perceptual, intellectual, personality, and social domains, and connected in its formation with the development of the organism as a whole. Second, it involves individual differences in process rather than content variables; that is to say, it refers to individual differences in the "how" rather than the "what" of behavior. Third, people's standing on the dimension is stable over time. It was because the articulated-global field-approach dimension was the most pervasive dimension of individual differences in cognitive functioning identified up to that time that we applied the designation cognitive style to it, rather than to the more specific field-dependence-independence (or flexibility-of-closure) dimension. A problem then cropped up, however. Because of the wide application of the field-dependence-independence label to our line of work, this distinction was soon lost in the literature. As a matter of custom, it became a common practice for authors (ourselves included) to refer to the more general dimension as field-dependent and field-independent cognitive styles, combining designations that originally had different referents.

A second problem our present conception confronts has arisen from our earlier usage of cognitive style. At issue here is the distinction between style and ability dimensions. While the term style has been given a variety of meanings in psychology, many of the common definitions distinguish style from goal-attainment ability. English and English (1958), for example, define style as: ". . . the sum total of the details of behavior that influence the attainment of a goal comparatively little but that give to an individual or to a particular performance a characteristic, almost an identifying, manner" (p. 531).

Very early in our work, when the research was still limited to perception of the upright, the body-vs.-visual-field conception of the self-consistent individual differences we had observed fitted this definition of style. To be sure, field-independent people show more accurate perception in some situations, such as the RFT and BAT, but field-dependent people are more accurate in other situations, such as the RRT. While none of these situations is ordinarily encountered outside the laboratory, we assume that under normal conditions field-dependent people rely more on visual cues and field-independent people rely more on gravitational cues, just as they do when these referents are separated by experimental manipulation in the laboratory. In the real world, however, gravitational and visual cues usually provide congruent information about the location of the upright, and accuracy is achieved equally by both field-dependent and field-independent people. Thus, the field-dependence-independence dimension was conceived to concern manner of functioning but to have little to do with goal attainment. Later, however, when we began to refer to the articulated-global dimension as a cognitive style, our usage of the term, style, did not conform to the conventional definition, as pointed out by several writers (e.g., Kurtz, 1969; Wachtel, 1972).

The difficulties we have been considering, arising from past usages of field dependence-independence and cognitive style, are avoided in the model we now propose. In our current conception the most general dimension of cognitive functioning that has been identified is a dimension of individual differences in the extent of autonomy of external referents. In several ways this dimension may be seen to conform with the concept of style (manner of moving toward a goal) rather than the concept of ability (competence in goal attainment). Because the labels field dependent and field independent have come into wide usage in connection with this line of work, we have also chosen to transfer these labels to the higher-level dimension of extent of autonomy of external referents.

As we have seen, field-dependent people, compared with field-independent ones, give more evidence of interpersonal competencies; in contrast, field-independent people have greater skill in cognitive restructuring. This suggests that the field-dependence-independence dimension is bipolar with regard to level, in the sense that it does not have clear "high" and "low" ends. Its bipolarity makes the dimension value-neutral, in the sense that each pole has qualities that are adaptive in particular circumstances. Evidence of the value-neutral character of the field-dependent and field-independent cognitive styles has become available from many sources, including a variety of real-life settings (Witkin, 1978). One particularly cogent source is the extensive research on the relation between field dependence-independence and educational-vocational preferences, choices, and performance (e.g., Quinlan and Blatt, 1972; Witkin, Moore, Goodenough, and Cox, 1977; Witkin, Moore, Oltman, Goodenough, Friedman, Owen, and Raskin, 1977). That research suggests that people are likely to favor and do better in educational-vocational domains to which their cognitive styles suit them. A second rather striking example of the value-neutral character of the field-dependence-independence cognitive-style dimension will be given later when we examine studies that compared members of subsistence-level sedentary agricultural groups and migratory hunting groups with regard to field dependence-independence. We thus see that field dependence and field independence are not inherently "good" or "bad"; each style can be adaptive in a particular context.

Judged by social-desirability criteria prevalent in our culture, the field-dependence-independence dimension does not appear to have any value bias either. Thus, field-independent people show the usually valued characteristic of developed cognitive restructuring skills, but they also show such commonly less valued attributes as "rude," "inconsiderate," "manipulate people as a means of achieving personal ends," "cold." Field-dependent people, in contrast, while having less developed cognitive restructuring skills, show such desirable characteristics as "tactful," "warm," "accommodating," "accepting of others," "want to help others." From a pan-cultural perspective, those of the attributes listed that are viewed positively in our society may have negative connotations in other societies.

To our earlier characterization of cognitive styles as process variables, pervasive and stable in nature, we have thus now added the characteristics of bipolar with regard to level and neutral with regard to value. These last two characteristics make cognitive styles distinctly different from unipolar and value-loaded ability dimensions, and serve to bring the conception of cognitive styles into line with conventional definitions of style.[7]

The model we have outlined views the development of field dependence-independence as multilinear. It proposes that the greater openness of field-dependent people to external sources of information is likely to stimulate the development of interpersonal competencies, but does not encourage the development of cognitive restructuring skills. It proposes as well that the more autonomous functioning of field-independent people may foster the development of cognitive restructuring skills, but not the development of interpersonal competencies. In this perspective, the primary developmental investments of relatively field-dependent and field-independent people are seen as being made in different domains, so that their psychological growth is in effect channeled along different routes. It is in this sense that our conception of the development of field dependence-independence is multilinear. Real development occurs along both routes; there is no implication of "arrest in development" of the kind that unilinear conceptions carry. Our model proposes as well that cognitive styles, which are process variables, affect the development of ability patterns in interpersonal competencies and cognitive restructuring skills. Cognitive styles are thus conceived to express themselves in these abilities, and, accordingly,

[7]The cognitive-style conception we have proposed has implications for how an individual's standing on the field-dependence-independence dimension may best be assessed at this time. It would indeed be ideal if it turns out in the factor-analytic studies that tests such as the RFT and BAT tap the higher-order field-dependence-independence cognitive style directly. Pending such studies, the RFT and a sampling of tests of the lower-order constructs would appear to provide the most effective test battery. To represent the cognitive-restructuring domain, the EFT should surely be included because it is well standardized, has considerable construct validity, and its relation to tests of other constructs in our model is well documented. Adequate tests of interpersonal competencies need to be developed to allow the fullest sampling of the array of lower-order constructs.

these abilities may serve as means for the assessment of cognitive styles.

COGNITIVE STYLES, ABILITIES, AND INTELLIGENCE

While we believe it appropriate to describe field dependence-independence as a cognitive-style dimension, it is important to note that cognitive restructuring is defined as an ability dimension. All tests of restructuring, such as the EFT, require subjects to restructure problem materials if they are to earn high scores. A high score therefore reflects the subject's ability to meet this requirement.

The fact that cognitive restructuring is an ability dimension holds implications for its relationship with measures of intelligence. If there is a very general ability dimension (G), in factor-analytic terms, then some correlation between restructuring and other abilities may be expected. In fact, the evidence shows that disembedding ability is related to verbal comprehension ability, for example. We were able to locate 11 studies, using adults as subjects and with a composite *N* of 811, that examined the relation of vocabulary-test scores to EFT performance, and RFT performance as well. The mean correlation between vocabulary and EFT scores was significant but small: $r = .14$. While not zero, that value is much lower than the correlations in the .30-to-.60 range usually found among measures of spatial restructuring. Thus, the restructuring and verbal comprehension constructs show a relationship, though small in magnitude. If intelligence is defined in terms of general cognitive abilities, the restructuring dimension may be considered the expression of field independence in intellectual functioning.[8]

In the same set of 11 studies, the mean correlation between vocabulary and RFT scores was not significantly different from zero

[8]The issue of intelligence may also be considered from the standpoint of conventional IQ measures. The previously cited factor-analytic studies of Goodenough and Karp (1961) and Karp (1963) found that EFT, RFT, and BAT appeared on a Wechsler perceptual-organization factor, loaded by the Wechsler Block Design, Object Assembly, and Picture Completion Subtests, all of which require restructuring, but not on a verbal-comprehension factor (loaded by the Wechsler Vocabulary, Information, and Comprehension Subtests) or on an attention-concentration factor (loaded by the Wechsler Digit Span, Coding, and Arithmetic Subtests), neither of which involves restructuring.

(r = .04). Thus, the field-dependence-independence cognitive-style construct and the verbal-comprehension construct are unrelated. The absence of a relationship between field independence and verbal ability as expressed in vocabulary tests suggests that the relationship repeatedly found between field independence and restructuring ability cannot be accounted for on the basis of greater overall capability of field-independent over field-dependent people.

MOBILITY-FIXITY

The cluster of restructuring skills and the cluster of interpersonal competencies are associated with opposite poles of the field-dependent-independent cognitive-style dimension. Measures of the one cluster may accordingly be expected to bear an inverse relation to measures of the other cluster, as in fact they do.

While the tendencies for people to be relatively high in cognitive restructuring skills and low in interpersonal competencies (that is, field independent), or, conversely, to be relatively low in cognitive restructuring skills and high in interpersonal competencies (that is, field dependent) are the patterns commonly found, the magnitude of the inverse relation between restructuring and interpersonal competencies is sufficiently low to allow for the possibility that these patterns are not the only ones to be found, and that, once present, they may be changeable. Indeed, it seems reasonable to believe that, with appropriate life circumstances and educational experiences, people may acquire access to both cognitive restructuring skills and interpersonal competencies, whatever their standing on the field-dependence-independence dimension. Accordingly, though we may expect quite often to find people who with fair consistency show the particular cognitive and social characteristics in which a field-dependent or field-independent cognitive style typically expresses itself, we may also expect to find people who show the characteristics associated with both styles—that is, who have both cognitive restructuring skills and interpersonal competencies.

People who show the characteristics prototypical of a field-dependent style with a high degree of regularity we would designate as "fixed" with regard to their use of the characteristics associated with that style. Others are equally "fixed" with regard to their use of the characteristics of a field-independent style. Still others have access to the characteristics associated with both styles; these people we would designate as "mobile."[9]

Since mobility signifies greater diversity in the ways of functioning that are available to the person, it is more adaptive than fixity. In saying that it is better to be mobile than fixed, we are adding another value perspective to the one proposed earlier, which used as a referent the fit between the person's cognitive style and the requirements of the situation at hand. The two value perspectives are complementary. There are indeed circumstances where a field-dependent or field-independent mode of functioning is more adaptive and the person with the mode that suits the given circumstances is benefited by using it. The person who has access to the characteristics of both modes, however, has the potential for adapting to a wider array of circumstances, compared to the person who is fixed, whether in a field-dependent or field-independent mode.

The mobility-fixity concept suggests a specific perspective for training in the cognitive-style domain. That perspective, which derives from the bipolarity of the field-dependence-independence dimension, is different from the definition of training objectives inherent in unipolar ability dimensions, where helping the person move toward the high end of the dimension is the clearly desirable goal. Because each pole of the field-dependence-independence dimension has adaptive characteristics, supplementation of the characteristics the person already has, so as to equip him or her with both sets of characteristics, is clearly a training goal of preference in the cognitive-style domain. A number of studies, to be reviewed later, have made it quite clear that competence in cognitive restructuring dimensions may be enhanced through appropriately designed educa-

[9]We follow the dictionary usage of the terms "mobility" and "fixity": "movable" vs. "nonmovable" or "set." These terms have been used in psychology in similar senses, though carrying additional specific connotations beyond those intended in our use of them (e.g., Duncker, 1945; Werner, 1957). Other studies described as dealing with mobility-fixity have been reported in the literature but these too have used conceptions different from the one proposed here (e.g., Bloomberg, 1971; Botkin, 1973; Haronian and Sugerman, 1967).

tional programs. These studies contain some suggestions, as we shall see, that training in restructuring as a general competence may lead to improvement in the more particular skills into which restructuring enters (e.g., Dolecki, 1976; Hurwitz, Wolff, Bortnick, and Kokas, 1975). Training in interpersonal competencies would seem to be an equally realistic possibility. Systematic research on this point is a task that lies ahead, but impressionistic accounts of the effects of efforts such as group encounter programs provide encouragement as to this possibility. For what it can accomplish in providing the individual with more diverse ways of coping, the development of mobility is an objective well worth striving for.

3

ORIGINS OF THE FIELD-DEPENDENT AND FIELD-INDEPENDENT COGNITIVE STYLES

We now examine the influences that may direct development toward a more field-dependent or a more field-independent cognitive style, both with respect to individuals during ontogeny and to groups over the course of cultural transitions.

In view of the different adaptive consequences of the field-dependent and field-independent modes of functioning, it seems reasonable to expect that they would be broadly tuned to the adaptive requirements of life circumstances among both individuals and cultural groups. In the sections that follow we consider, first, the course of ontogenetic development, second, how this tuning may be accomplished during the life history of the individual, and, finally, the historical course of human cultural development in relation to the adaptive aspects of the field-dependent and field-independent cognitive styles.

Development of Field Dependence-Independence During Ontogeny

The characteristic sequence in individual development is clearly from a field-dependent to a field-independent mode of functioning. Both cross-sectional and longitudinal studies of perception of the upright have shown a progressive decrease in the effect of the visual field, and increasing reliance on the body as a referent, until about the midteen years, with little further change during the years of maturity (e.g., Witkin et al., 1954; Witkin et al., 1962; Witkin, Goodenough, and Karp, 1967). Evidence available on cognitive restructuring skills shows a similar developmental trend (e.g., Maccoby and Jacklin, 1974; Witkin et al., 1962). Moreover, it is obvious that children function less autonomously of others in interpersonal relations than do adults.

Beyond these group trends, it is clear that individual differences in field dependence-independence and in cognitive restructuring ability are to be found at every age beginning as early as the kindergarten and preschool periods (Coates, 1975; Coates, Lord, and Jakabovics, 1975; Dreyer, Dreyer, and Nebelkopf, 1971). Individual differences have been found in development toward greater field independence, and children who develop rapidly toward field independence develop greater competence in cognitive restructuring. Because of their greater autonomy, we assume that such children are not as likely to have the extensive experience in interpersonal relations that foster the development of interpersonal skills among field-dependent children.

The evidence also suggests some differences in development of field dependence-independence among boys and girls in Western cultures. It is well known that, among adults, males tend to be more field independent than females on the RFT (e.g., Witkin et al., 1962). Sex differences have not been found as consistently on the BAT, but few studies have been done with this test because of the elaborate equipment it requires. Adult males do tend to score higher than females on many tests of restructuring skills, however (e.g., Maccoby and Jacklin, 1974; Witkin et al., 1962). Social-interpersonal skills may also be higher among women than men (e.g., Tyler, 1965), but this conclusion is not accepted by all authorities (e.g., Maccoby and Jacklin, 1974).

With specific reference to trends in the development of restructuring skills, the evidence suggests that pronounced sex differences in spatial-visualization ability, one of the specific restructuring abilities, emerge only during adolescence, with boys' superiority increasing through the high school years (e.g., Maccoby and Jacklin, 1974).

The course of development of sex difference in disembedding ability may be similar to that of spatial-visualization ability (Maccoby and Jacklin, 1974). The data on this issue are more difficult to interpret, however, because the rapid development of disembedding skill during the growth years has led to the use of different tests at different ages. Thus, the Preschool EFT (Coates, 1972) has been used almost exclusively for children below the age of six, and there is some indication of sex differences in favor of young girls on this test (e.g., Coates, 1974).

The Children's EFT (Karp and Konstadt, 1971) has most often been used for preadolescent school children. Although most studies have found that males tend to score higher than females on that test in this age period (e.g., Clack, 1970; Eddy, 1974; Finley and Solla, 1975; Stanes and Gordon, 1973), the differences are very small and usually not significant. A great variety of embedded-figures types of tests have been used with adolescents and adults, with marked differences in results among tests. On the individually administered EFT, mean scores typically tend to be higher for men than for women (e.g., Witkin et al., 1962), but sex differences are very small for group forms of the test, and usually significant only for very large samples (e.g., Dickie, 1969; Doherty, 1968; Nedd and Gruenfeld, 1976; Renzi, 1974). In view of the variation in results among tests with adults, and the use of different tests for different age groups, it is difficult to draw any definite conclusions about trends in the development of sex differences in disembedding ability.

For the RFT the developmental picture is quite clear. With few exceptions, studies of preadolescent school children have shown that boys tend to be more field independent on this test than girls (e.g., Dreyer, Dreyer, and Nebelkopf, 1971; Pearlstein, 1971). Furthermore, in our own cross-sectional and longitudinal studies, designed to span the age range from preadolescence (eight years) to young adulthood (17 years), no significant Age × Sex interaction was found on the RFT (Witkin, Goodenough, and Karp, 1967). These data indicate that on the RFT prominent sex differences emerge developmentally before puberty, in contrast to spatial-visualization and (possibly) disembedding abilities, and suggest a different origin of sex differences in perception of the upright than in cognitive restructuring.

There is also evidence from these studies that field dependence-independence may be established in a stable way fairly early in life. For example, RFT test scores for boys at age ten were substantially correlated with retest scores in the Witkin, Goodenough, and Karp study at ages 14 (r = .71), 17 (r = .72), and 24 (r = .66). Thus, cognitive styles in the later growth years and in early adulthood may be predicted with some accuracy from knowledge of cognitive styles in the prepubertal period.

In searching for the sources of the developmental changes, individual differences, and sex differences that have been described, we first examine the role of biological factors and then the role of training and of life experiences in the contexts of socialization, cultural encounters, and ecology.

Biological Factors in Ontogenetic Development

The finding that males tend to be more field independent than females has drawn attention to the possible roles of hormonal and sex-linked genetic factors in development of the field-independent and field-dependent cognitive styles.

HORMONAL DETERMINANTS

Historically, the most influential investigator of endocrine-cognitive relationships has been Broverman (e.g., Broverman, Broverman, Vogel, Palmer, and Klaiber, 1964; hereafter, Broverman et al., 1964; Broverman, Klaiber, Kobayashi, and Vogel, 1968; hereafter Broverman et al., 1968). Broverman and his colleagues have focused on two sets of cognitive situations. One set is called "automatization" tasks, and is characterized by the requirement that simple repetitive responses be rapidly emitted. The other set is called "restructuring" tasks, and is characterized by the requirement that salient stimulus attributes or overlearned responses be inhibited. Restructuring ability is often measured by a composite score on disembedding and spatial tests, and it should be obvious that our restructuring construct is very similar to Broverman's. Broverman combines these two sets into a single ipsatized, bipolar, cognitive-style dimension. We wish to focus on restructuring, however, since it has been much more widely studied by other investigators, it has more substantial construct validity, and it is closely related to field dependence-independence theoretically and empirically.

Two key propositions about the relationship between gonadal hormones and restructuring ability may be traced to the work of Broverman and his colleagues. One proposition is that androgen or estrogen affect the patterning of cognitive abilities (e.g., Broverman et al., 1968). In this view, when circulating gonadal hormone levels are high, performance on automatization tasks improves and performance on restructuring tasks declines. The biochemical theory advanced by Broverman and his colleagues in support of this idea has been severely criticized (e.g., Parlee, 1972; Singer and Montgomery, 1969), but whatever the biochemical basis for the linkage between androgen-estrogen levels and cognitive functioning, the idea has served to stimulate a great deal of research.

The second proposition is that late maturers have greater restructuring ability than early maturers (Broverman et al., 1964). This proposition has been further developed and elaborated more recently in connection with field-dependence theory by Waber (1976, 1977a, 1977b). The idea here appears to be that hormonal increases associated with the onset of puberty result in an arrest in development toward greater restructuring ability. This model seems analogous to the arrest in height development with gonadal hormone production during adolescence. Waber has suggested that pubertal onset affects the development of hemispheric lateralization, which in turn may affect cognitive restructuring ability.

The hypothesis that circulating androgen levels influence cognitive performance has been tested most directly by Klaiber, Broverman, Vogel, Abraham, and Cone (1971), who studied the effect of infused testosterone on automatization. Testosterone injections improved performance on simple repetitive tasks. Unfortunately, however, measures of restructuring ability were not included in this study. Thus, while these data suggest that speed of performance is increased by circulating androgen, they are not clearly relevant to our subject.

A more relevant study by Klaiber, Broverman, and Kobayashi (1967) related 24-hour urinary 17 ketosteroid (17KS) excretion to scores on various cognitive tests. They found that 17KS excretion was negatively correlated with scores on restructuring tests. Since high androgen levels result in greater 17KS excretion, these authors conclude that testosterone impairs restructuring ability. These results are suggestive. However, it should be noted that urinary 17KS does not constitute a very satisfactory estimate of testicular function, since 70 percent of the urinary 17KS comes from the adrenal glands and reflects metabolic products and precursors other than testosterone.

Moreover, a recent study with direct assessment of testosterone levels in adult males by radioimmunoassay techniques (Komnenich, Lane, Dickey, and Stone, 1978) failed to find any significant relationships with restructuring test performance within or between subjects. These results are not very definitive because of the small number of subjects involved, and because it is not clear whether fluctuations in testosterone levels from day to day were sufficiently large to expect much of an effect on cognitive functioning. They do raise questions about Broverman's interpretations, however.

Several studies have examined the relationship between measures of restructuring ability and physical indices of androgen functioning in adult males. In the first of these studies, Broverman et al. (1964) observed that subjects with low restructuring ability were more hirsute, wider and shorter individuals than subjects with high restructuring ability. Since these physical characteristics are known to be influenced by androgen production, these data tend to support the view of Broverman and his colleagues that restructuring ability is inversely related to androgen levels. Klaiber, Broverman, and Kobayashi (1967) also found a significant negative relationship between pubic hair development and restructuring ability. These data can be similarly interpreted. In subsequent studies, Rosenberg (1975) found that adult males who are broad shouldered and narrow hipped tend to do better than males who are narrow shouldered and broad hipped on a test of disembedding ability, but not on a test of spatial ability. Lawson (1977), however, found no significant relationships between masculinity indices of shoulder-hip width and restructuring tests of either type.

Petersen (1976) recently examined the relationship between spatial ability and the development of secondary sexual characteristics in a longitudinal sampling of adolescent males. Assessment of secondary sexual characteristics was based on ratings of muscle development, pubic hair distribution, genital size, and overall body build. For some of these indices, relatively more masculine physical characteristics were negatively related to spatial ability at ages 16 and 18, but not at age 13.

Rosenberg's (1975) study was the only one in this series of studies to include a measure of field dependence-independence in perception of the upright (RFT). No significant relationship was found with body build.

For females the evidence on relationships between physical signs of femininity and restructuring ability is not very clear, but hormonal functions are more complex in females and studies of women are still sparse (Lawson, 1977; Petersen, 1976; Rosenberg, 1975).

While the available evidence is not entirely consistent, it does suggest that males with more masculine physical characteristics are relatively low in cognitive restructuring ability, perhaps mediated by gonadal hormone production. If androgen levels are influential, however, it is not clear from these data whether the effect is current or is based on an historical association during earlier developmental periods.

The second proposition of Broverman et al. (1964) that individuals with low restructuring ability might be relatively early maturers was based on their observation that such subjects possessed relatively short, heavyset builds as adults, builds which tend to be characteristic of early onset of puberty. Waber (1976, 1977b) has subsequently pursued the notion that individual differences in spatial and disembedding abilities may be due to differences in maturational rates. She studied samples of early and late maturing adolescents as assessed by the Tanner criteria for identifying stages of development of secondary sexual characteristics. She found that, within each sex, late maturing individuals performed better on restructuring tasks than did early maturers. Late maturers also showed greater hemispheric lateralization for speech than early maturers, raising the possibility that the rate of maturation during adolescence may influence brain lateralization, which in turn determines the pattern of cognitive functioning.

The within-sex differences in pubertal age have also suggested the hypothesis that the male superiority in restructuring ability may be due to the later age of maturation in boys than girls (Waber, 1976; 1977a; 1977b). The fact that boys' superiority over girls' in spatial-visualization ability (and perhaps disembedding ability) becomes prominent only during adolescence also fits well with the idea that these abilities may show an arrest in development with pubertal onset. In this view, late maturers, who are more likely to be boys, may have a longer prepubertal period during which cognitive restructuring skills continue their rapid development.

It is important to note that Waber's finding of a relationship between restructuring abilities and maturation rates has not been replicated in subsequent studies. Neither Petersen (1976) nor Lawson (1977) were able to confirm this relationship. However, Waber's view does seem to account for a great variety of data, and, therefore, deserves a more extensive empirical test.

While it seems possible in the case of restructuring ability that individual differences in general, and sex differences in particular, may be affected by hormonal events during adolescence, this type of explanation may not apply to the field-dependence-independence dimension. As noted in the preceding section, prominent sex differences in RFT performance emerge before puberty, in contrast with the developmental trend in spatial-visualization ability. Moreover, the cognitive and personality correlates of RFT performance have been found in preadolescent children as well as in adults. These findings suggest that the origins of the field-dependent and field-independent cognitive styles lie in earlier developmental events.

It has been proposed that relatively high androgen/estrogen ratios during a critical period in the early life history of an individual may favor the development of a field-independent cognitive style (e.g., Dawson, 1972). Evidence for the hypothesis that early hormone levels may influence subsequent cognitive development has come from experimental research with animals on the effects of hormonal injections upon the use of spatial information in maze behavior (e.g., Dawson, 1972) and from studies of human pathological groups with an early developmental history of hormone abnormalities (e.g., Dawson, 1966; McGuire, Ryan, and Omenn, 1975; Money, 1968; Yalom, Green, and Fisk, 1973). Among these groups, the clearest results have been found in females with Turner's syndrome and in kwashiorkor males. Most studies have shown that Turner women, who are deficient in sex hormones during development, are relatively field dependent on the RFT and, though of normal verbal intelligence, are dramatically impaired on tests of spatial-visualization and disembedding ability (e.g., Money and Alexander, 1966; Nyborg, 1976; Serra, Pizzamiglio, Boari, and Spera, submitted; Shaffer, 1962). Kwashiorkor cases, who have low androgen/estrogen ratios during development, also show specific impairment on restructuring tasks, such as spatial-visualization tests (e.g., Dawson, 1966).

While it seems plausible to suppose that hormonal factors may play some role in the cognitive functioning of these groups, the fact that Turner and kwashiorkor cases are abnormal in many ways makes it difficult to rule out other possible biological and social explanations of the observed impairment. It is important, therefore, to ask whether groups with abnormally high levels of sex hormones or androgen/estrogen ratios in their early developmental history are superior in restructuring abilities. One study examined EFT and Block Design performance in patients afflicted with congenital adrenal hyperplasia, an abnormality involving high fetal androgen/estrogen ratios (McGuire, Ryan, and Omenn, 1975), but the number of cases was small and the results inconclusive.

A number of models have now been proposed to account for the data on endocrine-cognitive relationships. The most clearly worked through of these models assume that hormonal levels influence the development of hemispheric specialization of function at various ages during the growth years, which in turn affects the development of cognitive restructuring skills (e.g., Dawson, 1972; Waber, 1977a). These models appear to be consistent with differentiation theory. Much more research is needed, however, to clarify the basis of this relation and to determine whether hormonal levels are also related to other expressions of field dependence-independence.

GENETIC FACTORS IN FIELD DEPENDENCE-INDEPENDENCE

It has been proposed that spatial-visualization and disembedding abilities are influenced by an X-linked recessive gene (e.g., Bock and Kolakowski, 1973; O'Connor, 1943; Stafford, 1961); and several implications of the X-linked model have been tested to examine this possibility.

One kind of evidence has been sought in patterns of correlations between parents and children. Since fathers contribute their only X-chromosome to their daughters, and sons receive their only X-chromosome from their mothers, X-linked inheritance should produce relatively high correlations between members of opposite-sex parent-child pairs, and no correlation between fathers and sons. This pattern has been found for tests of spatial-visualization ability in some studies (Bock and Kolakowski, 1973; Hartlage, 1970; Stafford, 1961), but not in others (Carter, 1976; DeFries, Ashton, Johnson, Kuse, McClearn, Mi, Rashad, Vandenberg, and Wilson, 1976; Loehlin, Sharan, and Jacoby, 1978; McGee, 1978; Park, Johnson, DeFries, McClearn, Mi, Rashad, Vandenberg, and Wilson, 1978; Spuhler, 1976). In the case of the EFT, one early study found some marginal indication of higher relationships between members of opposite-sex than between members of same-sex parent-child pairs, as would be expected from an X-linked genetic model (Corah, 1965). This finding has not been supported by subsequent studies, however (Grunebaum, Weiss, Gallant, and Cohler, 1974; Oliver, 1974; Schaffer, 1969; Sholtz, 1973).

While the findings from most of these studies do not favor the X-linkage hypothesis, they do not necessarily warrant its rejection. Preadolescent children were used in some of the studies cited, and it is an open question whether X-linked genetic effects on these tests are to be expected before puberty. Moreover, it is possible that sex-role-modeling effects on the development of field dependence-independence (which we discuss in a later section) foster father-son and mother-daughter relationships that are different from and therefore obscure the pattern expected on a genetic basis. It may therefore not be possible to test the X-linkage hypothesis decisively with data on parent-child correlations.

Other implications of an X-linkage model have also been tested. One implication concerns the pattern of relationships between siblings. Since all sisters share the only X-chromosome their father has to contribute, but brothers may receive a different one of the two X-chromosomes their mother has to contribute, X-linked inheritance should produce higher correlations between sisters than between brothers. Some evidence of such a pattern has been found for spatial-visualization and disembedding abilities, but here again the results are not very consistent (e.g., Carter, 1976; Loehlin, Sharan, and Jacoby, 1978; McGee, 1978; Petersen, 1976; Yen, 1973). In addition, some evidence has been found that distributions of scores from several tests of spatial-visualization ability are bimodal, with frequency distributions that approximate a 50-50 division between the two groups of scores for men and a 25–75 split for women, as might be expected on the basis of an X-linked model (Bock and Kolakowski, 1973; Loehlin, Sharan, and Jacoby, 1978; Yen, 1973). Together these findings provide modest support for the hypothesis that there may be a major gene locus on the X chromosome, with recessive and dominant alleles, that contributes to individual differences in spatial-visualization ability.

Still other testable implications of the X-chromosome model lie in patterns of linkage to be expected among characteristics in transmission from parents to offspring. If two genes are located close together on the same chromosome, they tend to be transmitted together. Given a number of phenotypical characteristics that are known to be determined by genes spaced along the X chromosome (marker variables), this fact can be used to assess an X-linkage hypothesis. The model is relatively simple for transmission to sons, since sons receive only one X chromosome from their mothers. For mothers who are heterozygous with respect to a particular X-marker variable (i.e., their two X chromosomes bear different alleles at the gene locus), a pair of brothers who are similar to each other in the marker variable should also show greater similarity to each other in characteristics influenced by neighboring genes than a pair of brothers who differ from each other in the marker variable. Were sufficient marker variables available, the hypothesis that spatial-visualization, restructuring, or field dependence-independence have an X-linked determinant could be tested by analyses of similarities among brothers. Only a few practically useful X-chromosome markers are now known, however. As a consequence, a gene locus may be too distant on the X chromosome from any useful marker for linkage to be detectable. While linkage studies of this sort are not very sensitive as yet, there is no problem of interpretation should evidence of linkage be found. In fact, the data from one linkage study suggest that performance on both the EFT and RFT may be influenced by an X-chromosome gene located close to the locus for the Xg blood groups (Goodenough, Gandini, Olkin, Pizzamiglio, Thayer, and Witkin, 1977). Because the number of informative families was relatively small in that study, and no a priori hypotheses about specific gene loci were possible, its results are more suggestive than definitive, however.

In summary, it seems possible that some portion of the variance among people in restructuring ability is attributable to an X-linked genetic determinant, perhaps mediated by hormonal factors. This determinant may not extend to the level of field dependence-independence in our conceptual hierarchy, however. With the very limited evidence on hand, a definitive statement about the possible origins of field dependence-independence in the biological development of the individual—hormonal and genetic—is clearly not yet possible, but the concepts and findings already on hand suggest promising directions for further research.

Training, Child-Rearing, and Cultural Factors in Ontogenetic Development

Whatever future research may reveal about biological contributions to field dependence-independence and cognitive restructuring ability, it seems clear, from a large body of evidence already available, that environmental variables play a very important role in the development of these dimensions. A variety of environmental variables has now been studied, ranging from training programs designed to improve specific restructuring skills to child-rearing practices and cultural factors that may affect development of the broader characteristic of self-nonself segregation.

TRAINING

There is a growing literature on the contribution of training to performance on tests of spatial visualization, disembedding, and perception of the upright. The evidence from these studies suggests that the course of development in these dimensions may be affected by a variety of educational programs.[1]

The earliest studies of the influence of training on the EFT and RFT examined the effects of relatively brief periods of practice and/or instruction on the specific test performance the training was designed to improve (Gottschaldt, 1926; Witkin, 1948), and this line of work has been continued in a number of more recent studies (Elliott and McMichael, 1963; Goldstein and Chance, 1965; Klepper, 1969; Weiner, 1955; Wilkie, 1973). It is evident from these studies that performance on the EFT may be improved by practice with the test materials. Performance on the RFT may also be changed in a field-independent direction by focusing attention on body cues, or by learning to compensate for the illusory effect of the tilted frame. While these various training procedures affect test performance itself, it is doubtful that they alter the underlying perceptual functions of concern to us (Witkin, 1948). Extensive instructional efforts which result in transfer of training to other test materials than those used in the training clearly have more important implications for both theory and educational applications. We turn now to studies of such efforts.

One type of training study has been stimulated by reports that artists and musicians tend to be high in restructuring skills (e.g., Gaines, 1975; McFie, 1961; Trent, 1974; Witkin, Moore, Oltman, Goodenough, Friedman, Owen, and Raskin, 1977; Witkin, Oltman, Chase, and Friedman, 1971). Two factors may contribute to that relationship. First, field-independent people, who are characterized by highly developed restructuring skills and an impersonal orientation, may choose to

[1]The literature on training of spatial-visualization ability (e.g., Brinkman, 1966; Churchill, Curtis, Coombs, and Harrell, 1942) will not be reviewed in detail here.

enter, or be chosen for, art and music because these domains are especially compatible with their cognitive style (e.g., Witkin, Moore, Goodenough, and Cox, 1977; Witkin, Moore, Oltman, Goodenough, Friedman, and Owen, 1976). As an alternative, education in art and music may enhance restructuring skills. The latter interpretation seems plausible, since students in these fields are taught to analyze musical or artistic compositions. On the basis of correlational studies alone, however, it is difficult to know whether such training contributes anything to the greater field independence of artists and musicians. Experimental studies are now appearing in the literature, in which students assigned to special art or music classes are compared to untrained control groups with regard to post-training EFT performance (Hurwitz, Wolff, Bortnick, and Kokas, 1975; Leithwood and Fowler, 1971; McCord, 1973; McWhinnie, 1967, 1968, 1970b; Parente and O'Malley, 1975; Sutton-Smith, Baracca, Eadie, Mahony, and Zaren, 1977; Szeto, 1975). The results of these studies are not entirely consistent, but most have supported the training hypothesis.

A number of other studies have examined the effects of more specific perceptual training programs in which extensive general instruction is given in identifying and/or manipulating components of perceptual gestalten (Dolecki, 1976; Egeland, Wozniak, Schrimpf, Hage, Johnson, and Lederberg, 1976; McCarter, 1976; McWhinnie, 1967, 1968, 1970b; Reeves, 1971; Salome and Reeves, 1972; Szeto, 1975). Significant training effects on disembedding performance have been found in most of these studies. Three studies of the Sesame Street television series may also be added here, since one important section of the series involves gamelike demonstrations of perceptual analysis (Ball and Bogatz, 1970; Diaz-Guerrero and Holtzman, 1974; Salomon, 1973). Improvement in EFT performance among children who viewed the Sesame Street series has been found in each of these studies.[2]

[2]Training in simple sensory discrimination (Efland, 1965; Geffen, 1971; McCain, 1970), or general educational programs that may include discrimination training (Banta, 1966; Miller and Dyer, 1975), do not show consistent effects on measures on field dependence-independence; nor would field-dependence theory lead us to expect such effects.

Two examples of this line of work are worth considering in some detail because they employed well-documented curricula, and because they measured training effects with restructuring material that differed from the training material.

Dolecki (1976) studied the effects of the Project SEE training program (Knobler, 1971) on Piagetian conservation problems as well as on EFT performance. Project SEE is a perceptual, analytical training program designed for kindergarten and first-grade children. The period of instruction is 15 minutes per day, five days a week, for an entire academic year. During the sequence of class periods, instruction is given in the multidimensional analysis and reproduction of increasingly more complex visual training materials. The design of the study involved post hoc comparisons among three groups of students drawn from a large school district: one group that had received two years of SEE training (kindergarten and first grade), a second group that had received only one year of training (first grade), and a third group with no training. Significant one-year and two-year training effects were found on conservation and EFT performance both before and after covariance adjustments for a number of entry-level variables including reading readiness skills. These results are particularly interesting because they suggest a generalized enhancement of restructuring ability.

In another interesting study, Hurwitz, Wolff, Bortnick, and Kokas (1975) examined the effects of musical training by the Kodaly method (Kokas, 1969) on EFT performance. The Kodaly system emphasizes the development of skills in abstracting rhythmic and melodic constructions from folk music. The first-grade children in this study were given 40 minutes of daily Kodaly instruction in school, over a seven-month period. At the end of the training period they were significantly more field independent on the children's EFT than a control group of untrained children matched for age, intelligence, and social class. Here again, a generalized enhancement of restructuring ability is indicated.

The question may be raised as to whether these kinds of perceptual-analytical training programs also affect measures of field independence in perception of the upright. If restructuring ability is not involved in upright perception, as we have hypothesized, then training in restructuring skills should not transfer to the RFT or BAT. Unfortunately, only a few studies are available on this point as yet, and the results are conflicting (McWhinnie, 1970b; Parente and O'Malley, 1975).

Still another type of training study has been stimulated by the finding that field-independent people tend to have more developed athletic interests and skills (e.g., Elliott and McMichael, 1963; Meek and Skubie, 1971). Since body sensations are centrally involved in perception of the upright, one plausible hypothesis to account for such findings is that athletic training results in more field-independent performance on the RFT and BAT. This hypothesis has been examined in a few studies with occasional positive results, but the data on this point are inconsistent (David, 1975; Gill, Herdtner, and Lough, 1968; McCarthy, 1967). It has been reported that gymnastic training of children improves performance in figure-ground discrimination (Gill, Herdtner, and Lough, 1968) and identification of embedded figures (Leithwood and Fowler, 1971). If athletic training affects restructuring abilities as well as performance on tests of upright perception, then the training effects may exert their influence at a more general level in our conceptual hierarchy, perhaps even at the level of differentiation. The evidence available to date is far from definitive, but far-reaching implications for the theory of the development of differentiation, as well as for educational practice, would follow from a conclusion that athletic training transfers to a variety of restructuring tasks.

The training research reviewed in this section is still at an early stage, but the available evidence suggests that it may be possible to foster the development of cognitive restructuring skills by perceptual training in the manipulation of figure-ground relationships. These findings are exciting, not only because of their educational implications, but because, as noted earlier, a training approach may be used to examine the theory of field dependence experimentally. If there is a general dimension of restructuring ability that affects performance in a variety of cognitive tasks of disembedding, spatial-visualization, etc., as our hierarchical model suggests, and if general restructuring skills may be taught in appropriate training programs, then transfer of training should be expected throughout the range of restructuring tasks. While the evidence available at this time shows some generalizability, the range of restructuring behaviors to which training effects may transfer is still uncertain. For this purpose, a wider selection of outcome measures is needed than has been used thus far. In addition, much more needs to be known about how to maximize training outcomes; the critical features that characterize the effective training program have not yet been clearly defined. Studies are now needed that compare a variety of curricular material to test more specific hypotheses about training effectiveness.

Beyond all this, research is required on the effects of training upon the expressions of field dependence-independence in interpersonal competencies and autonomy in interpersonal relations. Both common experience and the apparent effects (usually reported in anecdotal form) of practically oriented programs of training in interpersonal behavior suggest that the social aspects of field dependence-independence are amenable to training.

Through the various lines of research proposed it may become possible to help people acquire the characteristics associated with both a field-dependent and field-independent mode of functioning, making for mobility in access to the characteristics in which these styles express themselves, as discussed earlier. Additional evidence on these issues may contribute to the further development of field-dependence theory, as well as to the attainment of practical educational goals.

CHILD-REARING PRACTICES

To this point we have been concerned primarily with the effects of training in perception of the upright and cognitive restructuring on the development of these components of field dependence-independence. We turn now to influences of a more general kind, likely to affect development at the higher level of self-nonself segregation in the differentiation model.

Our very early work on socialization (Witkin et al., 1962) led us to hypothesize that child-rearing practices that encourage separate autonomous functioning foster the development of differentiation, in general, and, more particularly, of a field-independent cognitive style. In contrast, child-rearing practices that encourage continued reliance on parental authority are likely to make for less differentiation and a more field-dependent cognitive style. It is not difficult to see how stress on adherence to external standards and continuous reinforcement of such an orientation during growth would work against the emergence of a self that is differentiated from others. On the other hand, stimulating the formation of internalized frames of references, arrived at through the individual's own experience, may plausibly be expected to work in favor of the self-nonself segregation.

These hypotheses about socialization practices were suggested in exploratory studies of child-rearing practices and attitudes of mothers of boys who were relatively field-dependent and field-independent, as defined by RFT, BAT, and EFT performance (Dyk and Witkin, 1965; Witkin et al., 1962). Interviews with these mothers identified several ways in which they were different in their handling of the separation issue. More commonly found among mothers of field-dependent than field-independent boys were attitudes and rearing procedures likely to encourage continued connections with her, such as limiting the child's activities in the community; emphasizing conformity; discouraging assertive and aggressive behavior, particularly when directed toward herself; and not stimulating the child to assume responsibilities.

Another observation made in this early exploratory study was that parents of field-dependent children more commonly used severe training as means of controlling their children than did parents of field-independent children. This impression was obtained from interviews with the mothers and from their children's TAT productions. In their TAT stories, relatively field-dependent children, more than field-independent ones, portrayed parental figures as punishing children, forcing them to do things they did not want to do, or preventing them from doing things they wanted to do.[3]

[3]It was already clear in very early studies that encouragement of separate functioning was not better or worse than encouragement of continued connectedness, with regard to their effects on the child's mental health. When psychological problems developed in children socialized by these two approaches, however, the problems appeared to be different.

These early exploratory studies stimulated considerable research on the role of socialization in the development of field dependence-independence, using a variety of methods and a wide range of subject populations. The weight of this evidence is consistent with the early hypothesis that socialization practices which encourage separation contribute to the development of greater field independence and restructuring ability.

One approach to the study of parental behavior has sought retrospective information about childhood experiences from subjects themselves. The results obtained with this approach are often lacking in detail, but because it is economical to use, it has been frequently employed, particularly in cross-cultural studies. Although studies using this approach have not been entirely consistent in outcome, they have shown, for the most part, that parental strictness in socialization is associated with children's field dependence and/or low disembedding ability in a wide variety of cultures. The subject populations used in these studies have included Americans, Temne and Mende of Sierra Leone, Eskimo, Hong Kong Chinese, West Indians, Zulus, Mexicans, and Trinidadians (e.g., Abelew, 1974; Baran, 1971; Berry, 1966; Bruner, 1977; Dawson, 1967a, 1967b; Dawson, Young, and Choi, 1974; MacArthur, 1970, 1971; Maloney, 1974; Mebane and Johnson, 1970; Nedd and Schwartz, 1977; Spuhler, 1976; Vernon, 1965).

In a second approach to the study of socialization in the development of field independence and disembedding ability, information about the child-rearing experiences of subjects was obtained from the parents themselves by means of standardized questionnaires or interviews of varying degree of structure. General measures of parental attitudes toward child rearing have not shown consistent relations to children's EFT performance (e.g., Busse, 1969; Claeys and DeBoeck, 1976; Domash, 1973; Hauk, 1967; Lee, 1974; Ribback, 1957). On the other hand, measures from questionnaires or interviews that included questions about parents' actual behavior toward their children have usually related significantly to the cognitive performance of their children (Claeys and DeBoeck, 1976; Edgerton, 1975; Irving, 1970; Jones, 1975; Kostlin-Gloger, 1974; Ramirez and Price-Williams, 1974a; Seder, 1957; Tendler, 1975). In most of these studies, questions concerned with autonomy and extent of encouragement or discouragement of separation distinguished between parents of relatively field-dependent and/or low restructuring children, and field-independent and/or high restructuring children.

The earliest and most elaborate of these studies compared parents of ten-year-old boys and girls with high and low EFT scores, matched for intelligence (Seder, 1957). Consistent with the results of our own early study, Seder found that children with low disembedding ability, more than children with high disembedding ability, were subjected to coercive child-rearing practices that stressed conformity and authority; had standards set for them by their parents; and were punished for assertive and aggressive behavior.[4]

In still another approach to the study of child-rearing practices, direct observations were made of parents' interactions with field-dependent and field-independent children. Several of these studies examined helping or teaching behavior of parents while their children were working on laboratory tasks. Two hypotheses have been addressed in these studies. One hypothesis is that parents of field-dependent children will be more strict and dominating than parents of field-independent children. The other hypothesis, based on a training perspective, is that parents of field-dependent children are less constructive in their teaching behavior than parents of field-independent children. Some evidence has been reported for each of these hypotheses.

With respect to the domination hypothesis, Busse (1969) found that mothers of children with low disembedding ability issued more commands than mothers of children with high dis-

[4]The observation by Seder (1957) and Witkin et al. (1962) that parents of field-dependent children are more likely to socialize against the expression of aggressive behavior than parents of field-independent children may account for the finding in a number of studies that field-independent people are able to express feelings of hostility and aggression directly against others, whereas field-dependent people characteristically avoid expressing hostility in this form (e.g., Bercovici, 1970; Dengerink, O'Leary, and Kasner, 1975; Greenfield, 1969). The use of strict disciplinary procedures by parents of field-dependent children may also be related to the observed tendency of such children to be particularly responsive to negative reinforcement in learning situations (e.g., Bell and McManis, 1968; Duvall, 1969; Randolph, 1971; Wade, 1971).

embedding ability. In another study, by Laosa (1976), Mexican-American and Anglo-American mothers were observed teaching their children to reproduce a tinker-toy model. Anglo-American mothers of children with low disembedding ability issued more commands, compared to mothers of children with high disembedding ability; and Mexican-American mothers of children with low disembedding ability showed more control of children's behavior than did Mexican-American mothers of children with high disembedding ability.

With respect to the training hypothesis, a study of mother-child dyads from Kenya (Kirk and Burton, 1977) found that mothers of children who did well on the EFT used more task-related gestures, and a greater proportion of these gestures were specific single-finger or single-hand movements. Several other observational studies produced less consistent results, however (Johnston, 1974; Sholtz, 1973). While some teaching-helping behaviors were found to occur more frequently among parents of children with high disembedding ability, others did not.

One problem with studies of this sort is that both constructive training and domination may be expressed in the same behavioral dimension. This problem is highlighted by the results of Busse (1969) who found a nonlinear relation between amount of parental manipulation of the task material and EFT scores of the child. Parents of children with high disembedding ability showed average amounts of manipulation, while parents of children with low disembedding ability either manipulated very little (suggesting that they were not very helpful in training) or very much (suggesting that they took the task over from the child).

Other observational studies have considered the family as a whole, focusing particularly on the power structure within families of field-dependent and field-independent children, as assessed by indices of participation, initiation, termination, and interruption, in conversations among family members recorded in the home and/or in the laboratory. In one study (Dreyer, 1975) the parents of field-dependent children (RFT and EFT) strongly dominated family interactions, whereas in families of field-independent children, power relations varied more from situation to situation and were less stringently structured.

Another study of mother-child conflict resolution in a role-playing situation found no significant relationship between assertive maternal behavior and field dependence of children, however (Hoppe, Kagan, and Zahn, 1977).

Still another observational study examined parent-infant interactions in relation to the child's level of field independence and disembedding ability in later childhood (Dyk, 1969). This longitudinal study is of particular interest because it suggests that socialization practices influencing the development of field dependence-independence may be operative very early in life. Mothers of children who became field dependent or field independent at six to nine years of age were different in the comforting methods they used in response to distress in their infants. Mothers of infants who developed a relatively field-dependent cognitive style were more likely to use nonspecific modes of comforting, dictated by the mother's own rather than the baby's needs, and they were prone to be repetitive in their comforting modes from one comforting occasion to another. It seems plausible to imagine that the infant who receives specific feedback, which varies with each of its inner states, is helped to identify and discriminate among needs and feelings within itself, and hence to develop a self that may become an effective referent for behavior.

A second longitudinal study carried out from infancy was done with a small number of cases among the Logoli people in East Africa (Munroe and Munroe, 1975). Infants whose mothers showed longer latency in response to their infants' crying were significantly higher in disembedding ability around five years of age than infants whose mothers responded quickly. The investigators suggest that the infant who is allowed to cry longer in what they describe as a society of normally "rapid baby responders" may begin to develop independence early. This difference was not found by Dyk (1969) among American children.

We consider finally the question of differences between maternal and paternal roles in the rearing of field-dependent and field-independent boys and girls. Much of the research on this question has been designed to explore the possibility that sex differences in field dependence-independence may be due to sex-role modeling, but it is relevant to socialization of self-nonself segregation as well.

In Western societies and many other cultures, the male sex role carries greater autonomy than the female sex role. Through socialization this sex-role difference may be transmitted from one generation to the next. Moreover, as we shall see in a later section, a persuasive case has been made by Berry (1966) and Van Leeuwen (1978) that sex differences in measures of field dependence-independence and restructuring ability are likely to be pronounced in cultures where sex roles are markedly different and socialization of sex-role stereotypes is emphasized. To the extent that children identify more with the same-sex than with the opposite-sex parent, sex-role modeling may be a major factor in the development of sex differences in field dependence-independence, as has been hypothesized by Lynn (1962, 1969), for example. If so, children (especially boys) of fathers who do not enter actively into the child-rearing process are likely to be relatively field dependent, and children (especially girls) of mothers who do not enter actively into the child-rearing process are likely to be field independent.

Some evidence for this hypothesis has been reported by MacEachron and Gruenfeld (1978). Among daughters, they found that greater paternal influence in family decisions was associated with greater field independence, while greater maternal influence was associated with greater field dependence.

The father's role has been examined in numerous studies comparing children from intact families with children from families in which the father was absent for various periods during the child-rearing years (e.g., Barclay and Cusumano, 1967; Lee, 1974; Louden, 1973; Schooler, 1972; Trent, 1974; Wohlford and Liberman, 1970). The weight of the evidence from these studies indicates strongly that father absence leads to greater field dependence and lower disembedding ability among boys, and among girls as well. There is also a variety of data on the father's role in intact families. Most of this evidence is consistent with the conclusion that families with strong paternal involvement are more likely to have sons who are field independent and have relatively high disembedding ability than will families with weak or inattentive fathers (e.g., Busse, 1969;

Dawson, 1967b; Dershowitz, 1971; Dreyer, 1975; Meizlik, 1973).

Another indication that a mother-salient surround is associated with lesser development of disembedding ability is the finding of Dawson (1967a, 1967b) that in the polygamous African families he studied, the greater the number of fathers' wives, the less disembedding ability among the sons. It seems likely that the more numerous his wives, the more limited is the father's relation to any one of his children.

Still another relevant observation is the association found between an extended family structure and field dependence and low disembedding ability, on the one hand, and a nuclear family structure and field independence and high disembedding ability, on the other (e.g., Claeys and Mandosi, 1977; Holtzman, Diaz-Guerrero, and Swartz, 1975; Witkin, Price-Williams, Bertini, Christiansen, Oltman, Ramirez, and van Meel, 1974). It is characteristic of the extended family for the grandmother to enter actively into the child-rearing process, thereby making the female role larger than in the typical nuclear family. Moreover, as we shall see in further detail later, cultures that provide a mother-salient surround are likely to be associated with the development of a field-dependent cognitive style.

The effect of maternal absence has been examined in only a few studies and the results have not been consistent (Schooler, 1972; Trent, 1974). There is evidence from intact families, however, that girls who identify less with their mothers (Bieri, 1960; Constantinople, 1974; Nilsson, Almgren, Kohler, and Kohler, 1973), or who view their mothers as more rejecting (Minkowich, 1967), tend to be relatively field independent and have relatively high disembedding ability.

While a sex-role modeling explanation may account for much of the evidence just reviewed, it also seems possible to account for the evidence by assuming that the father's active participation in child rearing may facilitate the child's separation from the nurturing mother, and thereby provide greater opportunity for autonomous development. There is evidence, for example, that mothers of father-absent families are likely to have particularly protective attitudes toward their children (e.g., Biller,

1971; Lee, 1974); and we may suppose that similar maternal attitudes are likely to exist in intact families in which the father's role is weak. Moreover, to the extent that fathers participate more in raising their sons than their daughters, separation from mother may be facilitated for boys, thus fostering the development of greater field independence among them.

Because the modeling and facilitation-of-separation views of the paternal role lead to similar outcomes, it is difficult to choose between them. Both views, however, imply that socialization plays an important role in the development of sex differences in field dependence-independence.

The weight of the evidence from each of the approaches discussed above is consistent with the conclusion that family environments which encourage separate functioning in children are likely to produce children who develop in the direction of greater field independence. Further support for this conclusion will be found in subsequent sections, where we examine the role of cultural and ecological factors in the development of field dependence-independence.

CULTURAL INFLUENCES

Evidence on the contribution of the social setting to the development of field dependence-independence comes from a quite recent but already large body of cross-cultural research. This research, reviewed in detail elsewhere (Witkin and Berry, 1975), has followed the strategy of comparing cognitive styles of groups showing a contrast with regard to the social arrangements and social standards conceived as relevant to the development of self-nonself segregation, and thereby, of a more field-dependent or field-independent cognitive style. These cross-cultural studies were undertaken with the hypothesis that members of societies that strongly emphasize conformity would be relatively field dependent, since stress on conformity discourages the development of separate autonomous functioning, and that they would thus be low in restructuring ability. In contrast, members of societies in which there is a greater tolerance of autonomy would be relatively field independent and better at restructuring. To put it in capsule form, the societies compared in these studies have differed in what Pelto (1968) has designated social "tightness" or "looseness." Societies at the tight end of the tight-loose dimension are characterized by an elaborate social structure, considerable role diversity, and pressure on the individual to conform with social, religious, and political authorities. Societies at the loose end have a less elaborate social structure, fewer roles, and individuals are allowed to "go their own way" to a greater extent. Since the primary means of achieving the result favored by society lies in socialization in the family, tight societies are characterized by stress on conformity to parental authority within the family and, with it, the use of strict and even harsh socialization practices. Moreover, in families of tight societies, the mother characteristically has a dominant role in the emotional and physical care of the child, whereas the father, while expecting respect and obedience from his children, participates little in these important areas. Thus, members of tight societies should be more field dependent than members of loose societies.

Studies conducted to check this hypothesis have examined groups differing in extent of social conformity with respect to both the field dependence-independence dimension and restructuring ability.[5] In these studies, and in the other cross-cultural studies to be reviewed in this and in subsequent sections, field dependence-independence was assessed almost always through RFT, but occasionally through BAT performance. Restructuring was assessed most often through performance on the EFT, Block Design, or the analytical triad of Wechsler subtests, and occasionally through articulation of the body concept (as judged from figure drawings), which we are now inclined to consider an expression of restructuring when the body itself is the object of experience (Witkin, Goodenough, and Oltman, 1979). The earliest studies with groups differing in extent of social conformity were conducted by Berry (1966), with the Temne and Eskimo, and by Dawson (1967a, 1967b), with the Temne and Mende. A great variety of different cultures, and subgroups within the same culture, have been compared in subsequent studies. In one study, for example, children from pairs of villages in each of

[5]The interpersonal-competencies component of field dependence-independence has received little attention in cross-cultural studies to date.

three countries—Italy, Mexico, Holland—were compared (Witkin, Price-Williams, Bertini, Christiansen, Oltman, Ramirez, and van Meel, 1974). In other studies, comparisons were made between Mexican and American children (Holtzman, Diaz-Guerrero, and Swartz, 1975; Tapia, San Roman, and Diaz-Guerrero, 1967); Colombian and American children (Lega-Duguet, 1977); Cuban and American children (Britain and Abad, 1974); Peruvian and American children (Gruenfeld, Weissenberg, and Loh, 1973); Mexican-American and Anglo-American children (e.g., Kagan, 1974; Kagan and Zahn, 1975; McGarvey, 1976; Naylor, 1971; Ramirez and Price-Williams, 1974b; Sanders, Scholz, and Kagan, 1976); Mexican-American and Anglo-American adults (Campbell, Crooks, Mahoney, and Rock, 1973); and subgroups from within Mexico (Ramirez and Price-Williams, 1974a). Still other comparisons have been made between the Pakeha and Maori (Brooks, 1976; Chapman and Nicholls, 1976); nomadic and sedentary groups in Pakistan (Berland, 1977); Jews of Middle-Eastern and Western origin, living in Israel (e.g., Amir, 1972, 1975; Kugelmass and Lieblich, 1975; Preale, Amir, and Sharan, 1970; Tannen, 1976; Weller and Sharan, 1971; Zadik, 1968) or in Europe (Rand, 1975); Jewish and Druze children living in Israel (Lifshitz, 1977); Jews and non-Jews in the United States (e.g., Adevai, Silverman, and McGough, 1970; Dershowitz, 1971; Radin, 1961; Wendt and Burwell, 1964); and Native American Indians and Anglo-Americans (Halverson, 1976). With a high degree of regularity, the results of these studies are consistent with the starting hypothesis relating field dependence-independence and restructuring ability to extent of stress on social conformity in the society.

The cross-cultural studies have also shed light on the sources of sex differences in field dependence-independence. These studies have shown that sex differences are more commonplace in tight-conforming than in loose-nonconforming societies (see Witkin and Berry, 1975; and Van Leeuwen, 1978, for recent reviews). The greater role diversity in tight than in loose societies, including more pronounced differences between male and female roles, the greater emphasis on autonomy in the socialization of boys than of girls, and the stricter enforcement of sex-role expectations, appear to be factors contributing to the more frequently found sex differences in tight societies.

In overview, the expectation that members of cultures and subcultures that are tight in their social organization and that stress social conformity would be more field dependent and less competent in restructuring than members of cultures and subcultures that have a loose social organization and place less stress on conformity has received substantial support from the studies reviewed in this section. Though most of the studies did not examine the socialization experiences of subjects themselves, in view of the characteristic child-rearing practices that are an integral component of tight-conforming and loose-nonconforming societies, these studies also lend support to the conclusion reached in the preceding section that child-rearing procedures that stimulate self-nonself segregation are likely to lead to a field-independent cognitive style. The ecocultural studies reviewed in the next sections provide still further support for that conclusion.

Ecocultural Factors in Cultural Adaptation and Ontogenetic Development

There is now a large body of evidence from studies of subsistence-level societies, recently reviewed by Witkin and Berry (1975) and Berry (1976), which indicates that members of nomadic hunting and gathering groups tend to be relatively field independent and to do well on restructuring tasks, as compared to members of sedentary agricultural groups. These findings may be viewed in both a contemporary and historical perspective. The issue of interest in the first perspective is the relation between the adaptive demands made on the individual by these contrasting ecologies and the development of a more field-dependent or more field-independent cognitive style during ontogeny. The issue of moment in the second perspective is the nature of changes in field dependence-independence over the course of human history.

Obviously, historical changes in field dependence-independence cannot be established directly. There is, however, indirect evidence to suggest a probable progression from a relatively field-independent to a relatively field-dependent cognitive style during cultural development since early times. We know from archeological evidence that, for most of their history, members of the human species were nomadic hunters and food gatherers, and that they learned to cultivate crops and domesticate animals perhaps only as recently as 8000 years ago. While there is clearly a limit to what can be determined from archeological evidence, we can learn something about the social structures, socialization practices, and cognitive styles that are most compatible with these contrasting economies from the nomadic hunter-gatherer and sedentary farmer-herder cultures in existence today. From this contemporary evidence it seems plausible to infer that as people moved from hunting to farming economies over the course of human history, the trend in development of cognitive style has been from field independence toward field dependence.

In the sections that follow we compare mobile hunting and sedentary agricultural groups, first with regard to ecological and culture features, and then with regard to cognitive style; subsequently, we consider how the inferred historical development from field independence toward field dependence may have come about.

ECOCULTURAL CHARACTERISTICS OF MIGRATORY HUNTING AND SEDENTARY FARMING ECONOMIES

Although subsistence-level groups with similar modes of economic exploitation of their environment have developed a variety of cultural forms, hunting and farming groups are typically different from each other in a number of important, interrelated ecological and cultural characteristics that may be viewed as products of their economic modes.

Demographically, hunters usually lead a nomadic life, following the game that provides their principal source of food. They travel in relatively small, often family-sized bands, limited in number by the capacity of the local game supply to meet their needs. In contrast, agriculturists lead a more sedentary existence, living in villages inhabited by the much larger population made possible by the increase in locally available food (e.g., Murdock, 1969).

Hunting and farming societies also differ in their tendency to accumulate food. Farming groups accumulate food in order to provide subsistence between harvest seasons. In contrast, the typical hunting group soon consumes most of its catch (e.g., Barry, Child, and Bacon, 1959).

Complexity of social structure also distinguishes hunting and farming groups. Migratory hunting societies are characteristically loose, with little permanent, centralized, political or religious authority beyond the family band. Farming societies are typically tight, with great diversity of social roles, marked social stratification, and an emphasis on compliance with social, political, and religious authority (e.g., Berry, 1976; McNett, 1970). The increase in group size and the need to regulate individual consumption between harvests have very likely contributed to the development of more complex and tighter social structures among agriculturists.

Still another difference between hunters and farmers is to be found in the nature of their socialization practices. As might be expected from their tight social structure, sedentary agricultural groups place great emphasis on obedience and compliance in child rearing. In contrast, child rearing in mobile hunting groups is usually characterized by greater emphasis on autonomy and self-reliance (e.g., Barry, Child, and Bacon, 1959).

Finally, hunting and farming groups differ in sex-role characteristics. In the smaller, mobile hunting society, with its limited role diversity, the contribution to the economy of women, along with men, is highly valued, with the consequence that obedience in women is not emphasized. In the larger, more complex societies of agriculturists, sex roles are more sharply distinguished and less value is placed on women's contribution; there is particular emphasis on obedience in female socialization (e.g., Berry, 1966; Van Leeuwen, 1978).

FIELD DEPENDENCE-INDEPENDENCE IN MOBILE HUNTING AND SEDENTARY FARMING SOCIETIES

From the characterizations just offered of nomadic hunting and sedentary farming societies, a field-independent cognitive style would appear to be more adaptive for the hunter, and a field-dependent cognitive style for the farmer. The activities involved in hunting and gathering often require self-reliance and autonomy. They also require the ability to extract key information from the surrounding field, usually homogeneous in character, in order to locate game and other food. Moreover, the hunter, in his mobile existence, must be continuously aware of his location in space if he is to return home safely. We may imagine, therefore, that cognitive restructuring skills are particularly adaptive in the life of the hunter-gatherer. In contrast, only minimal interpersonal competencies may be required in the hunter's relatively isolated life (e.g., Berry, 1966, 1976; Dawson, 1969; Witkin and Berry, 1975).

The typical agricultural group is very different in these respects. The more sedentary existence of its members places less demand on autonomy and cognitive restructuring skills. In contrast, social-interpersonal relationships are likely to be important in the larger social groups in which the farmer lives. It is easy to suppose that the interpersonal competencies of field-dependent people would be particularly adaptive in subsistence-level sedentary farming cultures (Witkin and Berry, 1975).

Given the apparent fit between the adaptive advantages of a field-independent cognitive style and the ecocultural characteristics of a nomadic hunting existence, on the one hand, and between the adaptive advantages of a field-dependent cognitive style and the characteristics of a sedentary-agricultural existence, on the other, it would not be at all surprising to find members of hunting societies to be more field independent than members of farming societies. The results of many studies with groups from widely different parts of the world give strong support for this expectation.

The most extensive evidence is provided by Berry (1976) in a study which, though only recently reported, has been in progress for some years. Berry combined the economic and demographic variables enumerated in the preceding section into a single ecocultural dimension, typified at one extreme by a nomadic hunting-gathering existence in small groups, and, at the other extreme, by a sedentary-agricultural existence in large settlements. He then examined members of seventeen different samples, ranged along the dimension of cognitive restructuring tasks, and in some instances on the RFT. The standing of these groups on the cognitive style dimension was in good agreement with their standing on the ecocultural dimension, in the direction predicted. Additional migratory hunting-gathering groups that have been examined in other more circumscribed studies include Canadian, Greenland, and Alaskan Eskimos, Newfoundlanders, and Labradorians (e.g., Berry, 1966; Brooks, 1976; Feldman, 1971; Jones, 1975; MacArthur, 1973, 1978; MacKinnon, 1972; Preston, 1964; Schubert and Cropley, 1972; Taylor and Skanes, 1976); Cree, Athabaskan, Ojibway, and Carrier Amerindians (e.g., Berry and Annis, 1974; Kane, 1973; St.John, Krichev, and Bauman, 1976; Weitz, 1971); Lapps (Forsius, 1973); the Australian Arunta (Berry, 1971; Dawson, 1969); Fijians (Bennett and Chandra, 1975); the Boat People of Hong Kong (Dawson, 1970); and the Bihars of India (Sinha, 1978). At the sedentary agricultural-gathering end of the ecocultural continuum, the groups studied have included the Temne and the Mende of Sierra Leone (Berry, 1966; Dawson, 1967a, 1967b); Southern Nigerians (Wober, 1967); Bantu-speaking South Africans (Baran, 1971); the Nsenga of Zambia (MacArthur, 1975); the Haka of Hong Kong (Dawson, 1970); Fijians (Bennett and Chandra, 1975; Chandra, 1974); Tsimshian Amerindians (Berry and Annis, 1974); and the Oraons of India (Sinha, 1978). Whereas the migratory-hunting gathering groups have most often been found to be relatively field independent and high in restructuring ability, the sedentary agricultural groups were commonly relatively field dependent and lower in restructuring ability.[6]

In view of the nature of the socialization practices represented at each end of the ecocultural dimension, the evidence from these studies provides further support for

[6]The hypothesis relating ecocultural variables to cognitive style was conceived as relevant in subsistence-level peoples only (Berry, 1976); and the evidence available in support of the hypothesis is limited to studies of such peoples alone. A good deal of recent work has been directed, however, at nonsubsistence level groups undergoing acculturation. A common finding in these studies is that the experience of education is related to field independence, particularly as manifested in cognitive restructuring skills (e.g., Berry, 1966; MacArthur, 1975; McFie, 1961; Wober, 1966). We have another indication here that particular training experiences may contribute to the development of field independence.

the conclusions reached earlier about the role of child rearing in the development of field dependence-independence. By implicating tight vs. loose social organization, these studies also add support to earlier conclusions about the role of cultural factors.

Many of the studies carried out from an ecocultural perspective also suggest that sex differences in field dependence-independence and restructuring ability vary with the mode of economic exploitation. Where sex differences have been found, they are largely from samples at the sedentary farming end of the continuum; they tend to be absent from samples at the migratory hunting end (Witkin and Berry, 1975; Van Leeuwen, 1978). In the economic mode, and its sequelae, we thus find an additional source of sex differences in field dependence-independence and cognitive restructuring.

Altogether, the results of the studies reviewed in this section clearly support the conclusion that, as expected, nomadic hunting people tend to be more field independent and higher in restructuring ability than sedentary farming people, and these differences are particularly pronounced between women in the two settings.

THE HISTORICAL DEVELOPMENT OF FIELD DEPENDENCE-INDEPENDENCE

Viewed from an adaptive standpoint, the interrelation among constituents of the contrasting clusters of economic, demographic, cultural, socialization, and cognitive-style variables found in hunting and farming societies in existence today seems eminently reasonable. To that extent, the inference that these same variables were similarly interrelated during the history of human cultural development also seems reasonable.

The proposal that the historic sequence was from relative field independence to relative field dependence, as societies moved from a hunting to a farming economic base, leaves open the question of how the change in cognitive style was brought about. In approaching this question, it seems plausible to suppose that a long history of living in the same ecological context, under the pressures of a subsistence level existence, would foster both cultural and biological adaptations to the demands of the ecology.

With regard to cultural adaptation, it is reasonable to believe that the adaptive social structures and socialization practices we have found to exist in nomadic hunting and sedentary farming groups today were the same ones favored over the long history of development of these groups. The ecological press thus provided an important early impetus, and a continuing guiding force, in the shaping of cultural forms, through phenotypic transmission, calculated to produce individuals capable of functioning in ways suited to their environment. Cognitive styles may clearly be included among the adaptive ways of functioning.

While biological factors may also have played some role in the evolution of individual cognitive styles, at the moment there is no evidence on this possibility. Several hypotheses may be considered, however.

One hypothesis, proposed by Dawson (1967b), is that the lesser protein intake of farmers—by lowering their androgen/estrogen ratios—may make them more field dependent than hunters.

Another hypothesis is suggested by some of the implications of the sex-linked recessive model of spatial-visualization ability examined in an earlier section. Genetic models do not usually lead to the expectation that a recessive allele will produce adaptive phenotypes. The sex-linked recessive model therefore poses a paradox: how, over the course of history, did an adaptive characteristic like spatial-visualization ability come to be favored by a recessive allele? This question has been addressed by Kolakowski and Malina (1974), who suggest that, in early peoples, greater spatial-visualization ability may have had adaptive consequences only for men because of their sex role as hunters. Since an X-linked gene has recessive-dominant properties only for women, this suggestion may be of some help in resolving the paradox. However, the model of Kolakowski and Malina cannot easily accommodate the finding that, whereas sex differences in spatial-visualization ability and other restructuring skills have been found in subsistence-level farming-herding cultures in existence today, there has been little evidence of sex difference in subsistence-level hunting groups (e.g., Witkin and Berry, 1975; Van Leeuwen, 1978). If an X-linked recessive gene is involved, these data could be accounted for by assuming that the dominant allele emerged during evolution from hunting to farming economies. The bipolar aspect of the field-dependence-independence model may then become useful in resolving the paradox by allowing the inference that a shift occurred in adaptive requirements from the restructuring skills associated with a field-independent cognitive style to the social skills (favored by the dominant allele) associated with a field-dependent cognitive style during the transition from hunting to farming economies. As we emphasized earlier, it is unclear at this time whether an X-linked recessive model in fact applies to the field-dependence-independence dimension. If future research indicates that it does, the implications of the assumption that the recessive allele emerged in the transition from hunting to farming economies could be tested empirically in studies of hunting and farming groups in existence today.

Whether or not there is a genetic contribution to individual differences in field dependence-independence, it is quite easy to account for the difference in cognitive style between hunting and farming groups on the basis of ecological, cultural, and socialization effects operating during the lifetime of the individual. There is an obvious and even dramatic correspondence between the autonomy-fostering socialization practices typically found in hunting societies and the child-rearing practices that foster the ontogenetic development of a relatively field-independent cognitive style within a given cultural group. In contrast, the socialization practices of the typical farming society, which encourage obedience and limit separation from parental authority, are similar to the child-rearing practices that are associated with the ontogenetic development of a relatively field-dependent cognitive style within cultures. Further contributing to the development of field independence and cognitive restructuring ability among hunters during their lifetime may be the opportunities available to them, as they engage in the search for game, for activities that encourage self-reliance and direct perceptual learning. Social structure, socialization experiences, and ecological encounters may thus work in tandem toward the same developmental goal of producing adaptive modes of behavior in the individual. Certainly, the results of cross-cultural comparisons of migratory hunting and sedentary farming groups are consistent with the conclusion reached in earlier sections that environmental factors operative during ontogeny play a key role in the development of individual differences in cognitive style.

The sex differences in field dependence-independence commonly found in sedentary farming societies, but rarely in nomadic hunting societies, are also readily explained on the basis of ecocultural factors at work during ontogenetic development. The greater distinctiveness of sex roles in agricultural societies, the lesser value placed on women's contribution to the economy, and the more limited opportunity for self-nonself segregation resulting from greater emphasis on obedience in female socialization, make development in a field-dependence direction particularly likely among women in such groups (Van Leeuwen, 1978).

In considering the relative contributions of cultural and genetic factors in the historic development of field dependence-independence, we may also note that, without doubt, cultural-transmission mechanisms in humans work more quickly and are much more important in producing change than genetic mechanisms (e.g., Cavalli-Sforza and Feldman, 1973a, 1973b). In this perspective the ecocultural changes that occurred in the transition to agricultural economies, under the impetus of a subsistence-level existence, may have been sufficient to produce the historical changes in the direction of greater field dependence that we have postulated.

Some developmental theories implicitly assume that developmental progressions proceed in the same direction during ontogeny and during the history of human adaptation (e.g., Werner, 1948). In contrast, field-dependence theory leads to a quite different expectation. Whereas ontogenetic development proceeds from a state of relative field dependence to a state of relative field independence, cultural development, we have suggested, follows an opposite course. That the developmental series may proceed in opposite directions in the case of a cognitive-style dimension is not surprising when we consider that the characteristics at each extreme of the dimension have adaptive value in different situations. As we have suggested, a field-independent cognitive style may have been particularly adaptive to the hunting-gathering existence of early people, whereas a field-dependent cognitive style may have been more adaptive to the sedentary existence of later agricultural groups. Similarly, reliance on external standards, characteristic of a field-dependent cognitive style, seems more suited to the physical and intellectual status of young children, whereas a greater degree of personal autonomy, characteristic of a more field-independent cognitive style, is better suited to adult status. An individual's cognitive style thus appears to be attuned to his capabilities and to the requirements of the environment with which he must cope.

Although the two developmental series may proceed in opposite directions, the question of how this attunement is accomplished may be understood within a single conceptual framework. As we have seen, there is evidence that specific training effects may contribute to the development of the cognitive-restructuring component of field independence during the life history of the individual, and it is likely that perceptual learning contributes to such a development among hunters through their nomadic existence and economic pursuits. Socialization practices that encourage separation from parental authority may contribute both to the ontogenetic development of a field-independent cognitive style within a cultural group, as well as to greater field independence among members of early hunting societies than among members of later farming societies. Although the contribution of biological factors to individual differences in field dependence-independence is not yet clear, these factors may also be relevant to both developmental series.

In the observation that movement toward field dependence may be favored in one developmental series, and movement toward field independence favored in another, we have an additional indication that the conception of development proposed by field-dependence theory is a multilinear one.

It is a major aim of cognitive-style theorists to seek unifying themes that cut across traditional areas of research on human behavior. We see this in field-dependence theory, which provides a means of bringing together within a common conceptual framework areas as diverse as the ones that have been examined in this monograph.

REFERENCES

Abelew, T. (1974), *Sex Role Attitudes, Perceptual Style, Mathematical Ability and Perceived Parental Child-Rearing Attitudes in Adolescents.* Doctoral dissertation, Fordham University. *Dissertation Abstracts International,* 35:1439B (University Microfilms No. 74-19,696).

Adevai, G., Silverman, A. J., & McGough, W. E. (1970), Ethnic Differences in Perceptual Testing. *International Journal of Social Psychiatry,* 16:237–239.

Adler, R., Gervasi, A., & Holzer, B. (1973), Perceptual Style and Pain Tolerance: II. The Influence of Certain Psychological Factors. *Journal of Psychosomatic Research,* 17:369–379.

Amir, Y. (1972), Inter- and Intra-Ethnic Comparisons of Intellectual Functions in Israeli and Middle Eastern Populations. *Abstract Guide of the Twentieth International Congress of Psychology,* Tokyo, 175–176.

______ (1975), Perceptual Articulation in Three Middle Eastern Cultures. *Journal of Cross-Cultural Psychology,* 6:406–416.

Antler, L. (1964), *Relative Effects of Field Dependence, Need for Social Approval and Stimulus Clarity upon Conformity.* Doctoral dissertation, Columbia University. *Dissertation Abstracts,* 25:7403 (University Microfilms No. 65-4569).

Asch, S. E., & Witkin, H. A. (1948a), Studies in Space Orientation. I. Perception of the Upright with Displaced Visual Fields. *Journal of Experimental Psychology,* 38:325–337.

______ & ______ (1948b), Studies in Space Orientation. II. Perception of the Upright with Displaced Visual Fields and with Body Tilted. *Journal of Experimental Psychology,* 38:455–477.

Austrian, R. W. (1976), *Differential Adaptation of Field Independent and Field Dependent Subjects to Therapy-Analogue Situations Varying in Degree of Structure.* Doctoral dissertation, New York University. *Dissertation Abstracts International,* 1977, 38:885B (University Microfilms No. 77-16,465).

Balance, W. D. G. (1967), *Acquiescence: Acquiescent Response Style, Social Conformity, Authoritarianism, and Visual Field Dependency.* Doctoral dissertation, University of Alabama. *Dissertation Abstracts,* 1968, 28:3458B (University Microfilms No. 68-1027).

Ball, S., & Bogatz, G. A. (1970), *The First Year of Sesame Street: An Evaluation* (ETS PR 70-15). Princeton, N.J.: Educational Testing Service.

Banta, T. J. (1966), *Progress Report: The Montessori Research Project.* Cincinnati, Ohio: University of Cincinnati.

Baraga, E. S. (1977), *The Relationship of Social and Maturational Variables to Development of Field-Dependence in Preschoolers: A Longitudinal Study.* Doctoral dissertation, University of North Dakota. *Dissertation Abstracts International,* 1978, 39:351B–352B (University Microfilms No. 78-10313).

Baran, S. (1971), *Development and Validation of a TAT-Type Projective Test for Use Among Bantu-Speaking People* (CSIR Special Report No. PERS 138). Johannesburg, South Africa: National Institute for Personnel Research, Council for Scientific and Industrial Research.

Barclay, A., & Cusumano, D. R. (1967), Father Absence, Cross-Sex Identity, and Field-Dependent Behavior in Male Adolescents. *Child Development,* 38:243–250.

Barrett, G. V., & Thornton, C. L. (1967), Cognitive Style Difference Between Engineers and College Students. *Perceptual and Motor Skills,* 25:789–793.

______ ______ & Cabe, P. A. (1970), Cue Conflict Related to Perceptual Style. *Journal of Applied Psychology,* 54:258–264.

Barry, H., Child, I. L., & Bacon, M. K. (1959), Relation of Child Training to Subsistence Economy. *American Anthropologist,* 61:51–63.

Beckerle, G. P. (1966), *Behavioral Traits Related to Psychological Differentiation in Pre-Adolescent Boys.* Doctoral dissertation, Michigan State University. *Dissertation Abstracts,* 28:336B. (University Microfilms No. 67-7519).

Bell, D. R., & McManis, D. L. (1968), Perceptual Differences of Subjects Classified as Reward Seekers and Punishment Avoiders. *Perceptual and Motor Skills,* 27:51–56.

Bennett, M., & Chandra, S. (1975), Some Ecological Factors in Individual Test Performance. In: *Readings in Cross-Cultural Psychology,* ed. J. L. M. Dawson & W. J. Lonner. Hong Kong: Hong Kong University Press, pp. 185–189.

Bercovici, A. M. (1970), *The Influence of Aggressive and Non-Aggressive Television and Cognitive Style on Elementary and Junior High School Children.* Unpublished master's thesis, University of California, Los Angeles.

Bergman, H., & Engelbrektson, K. (1973), An Examination of Factor Structure of Rod-and-Frame Test and Embedded-Figures Test. *Perceptual and Motor Skills,* 37:939–947.

Berland, J. C. (1977), *Cultural Amplifiers and Psychological Differentiation Among Khanabadosh in Pakistan.* Unpublished doctoral dissertation, University of Hawaii.

Berry, J. W. (1966), Temne and Eskimo Perceptual Skills. *International Journal of Psychology,* 1:207–229.

______ (1971), Ecological and Cultural Factors in Spatial Perceptual Development. *Canadian Journal of Behavioural Science,* 3:324–336.

______ (1976), *Human Ecology and Cognitive Style: Comparative Studies in Cultural and Psychological Adaptation.* New York: Wiley.

______ & Annis, R. C. (1974), Ecology, Culture and Psychological Differentiation. *International Journal of Psychology,* 9:173–193.

Bieri, J. (1960), Parental Identification, Acceptance of Authority, and Within-Sex Differences in Cognitive Behavior. *Journal of Abnormal and Social Psychology,* 60:76–79.

Biller, H. B. (1971), The Mother-Child Relationship and Father-Absent Boy's Personality Development. *Merrill-Palmer Quarterly,* 17:227–241.

Birmingham, D. L. (1974), *Situational and Personality Factors in Conformity.* Doctoral dissertation, Saint Louis University. *Dissertation Abstracts International,* 35:2421B (University Microfilms No. 74-24,042).

Blake, R. R., & Ramsey, G. V. (1951), *Perception: An Approach to Personality.* New York: Ronald Press.

Bloomberg, M. (1971), Creativity as Related to Field Independence and Mobility. *Journal of Genetic Psychology,* 118:3–12.

Bock, R. D., & Kolakowski, D. (1973), Further Evidence of Sex-Linked Major-Gene Influence on Human Spatial Visualizing Ability. *American Journal of Human Genetics,* 25:1–14.

Botkin. E. B. (1973), *Fixity-Mobility: Its Relationship to Field Independence and Rigidity.* Doctoral dissertation, Yeshiva University. *Dissertation Abstracts International,* 1974, 34:4653B–4654B (University Microfilms No. 74-7857).

Brandsma, J. M. (1971), *The Effects of Personality and Placebo-Instructional Sets on Psychophysiological Responding.* Doctoral dissertation, Pennsylvania State University. *Dissertation Abstracts International,* 32:6672B (University Microfilms No. 72-13,817).

Brinkman, E. H. (1966), Programmed Instruction as a Technique for Improving Spatial Visualization. *Journal of Applied Psychology,* 50:179–184.

Britain, S. D., & Abad, M. (1974), Field-Independence: A Function of Sex and Sociliazation in a Cuban and an American Group. Paper presented at the meeting of the American Psychological Association, New Orleans, September.

Brooks, I. R. (1976), Cognitive Ability Assessment with Two New Zealand Ethnic Groups. *Journal of Cross-Cultural Psychology,* 7:347–356.

Brosgole, L., & Cristal, R. M. (1967), The Role of Phenomenal Displacement on the Perception of the Visual Upright. *Perception and Psychophysics,* 2:179–188.

Broverman, D. M., Broverman, I. K., Vogel, W., Palmer, R. D., & Klaiber, E. L. (1964), The Automatization Cognitive Style and Physical Development. *Child Development,* 35:1343–1359.

——— Klaiber, E. L., Kobayashi, Y., & Vogel, W. (1968), Roles of Activation and Inhibition in Sex Differences in Cognitive Abilities. *Psychological Review,* 75:23–50.

Bruner, J. S., & Krech, D., Eds. (1950), *Perception and Personality: A Symposium.* Durham, N.C.: Duke University Press.

Bruner, P. B. (1977), *The Effects of Perceived Parental Nurturance, Sex of Subject, and Practice on Embedded Figures Test Performance.* Doctoral dissertation, Emory University. *Dissertation Abstracts International,* 1978, 38:3978B–3979B (University Microfilms No. 77-32,373).

Busch, J. C., & DeRidder, L. M. (1973), Conformity in Preschool Disadvantaged Children as Related to Field-Dependence, Sex, and Verbal Reinforcement. *Psychological Reports,* 32:667–673.

Busse, T. V. (1968), Establishment of the Flexible Thinking Factor in Fifth Grade Boys. *Journal of Psychology,* 69:93–100.

——— (1969), Child-Rearing Antecedents of Flexible Thinking. *Developmental Psychology,* 1:585–591.

Campbell, J. T., Crooks, L. A., Mahoney, M. H., & Rock, D. A. (1973), *An Investigation of Sources of Bias in the Prediction of Job Performance: A Six-Year Study* (ETS PR 73-37). Princeton, N.J.: Educational Testing Service (ERIC

Document Reproduction Service No. ED 073 121).
Carter, S. L. (1976), *The Structure and Transmission of Individual Differences in Patterns of Cognitive Ability.* Doctoral dissertation, University of Minnesota. *Dissertation Abstracts International,* 1977, 37:5318B–5319B (University Microfilms No. 77-7037).
Cattell, R. B. (1948), Primary Personality Factors in the Realm of Objective Tests. *Journal of Personality,* 16:459–487.
______ (1955), The Principal Replication Factors Discovered in Objective Personality Tests. *Journal of Abnormal and Social Psychology,* 50:291–314.
______ (1957), *Personality and Motivation Structure and Measurement.* New York: World.
______ (1963), Theory of Fluid and Crystallized Intelligence: A Critical Experiment. *Journal of Educational Psychology,* 54:1–22.
______ (1969), Is Field Independence an Expression of the General Personality Source Trait of Independence, U.I.19? *Perceptual and Motor Skills,* 28:865–866.
______ & Warburton, F. W. (1967), *Objective Personality and Motivation Tests: A Theoretical Introduction and Practical Compendium.* Urbana, Ill.: University of Illinois Press.
Cavalli-Sforza, L., & Feldman, M. W. (1973a), Cultural Versus Biological Inheritance: Phenotypic Transmission from Parent to Children. (A Theory of the Effect of Parental Phenotypes on Children's Phenotype.) *American Journal of Human Genetics,* 25:618–634.
______ & ______ (1973b), Models for Cultural Inheritance. I. Group Mean and Within Group Variation. *Theoretical Population Biology,* 4:42–55.
Cegalis, J. A., & Leen, D. (1977), Individual Differences in Responses to Induced Perceptual Conflict. *Perceptual and Motor Skills,* 44:991–998.
Chandra, S. (1974), Cognitive Development—Indians and Fijians. Paper presented at the Second International Conference of the International Association for Cross-Cultural Psychology, Kingston, Ontario, August.
Chapman, J. W., & Nicholls, J. G. (1976), Occupational Identity Status, Occupational Preference, and Field Dependence in Maori and Pakeha Boys. *Journal of Cross-Cultural Psychology,* 7:61–72.
Chomsky, N. (1965), *Aspects of the Theory of Syntax.* Cambridge, Mass.: MIT Press.
Churchill, R. D., Curtis, J. M., Coombs, C. H., & Harrell, T. W. (1942), Effect of Engineer School Training on the Surface Development Test. *Educational and Psychological Measurement,* 2:279–280.
Clack, G. S. (1970), *Effects of Social Class, Age, and Sex on Tests of Perception, Affect Discrimination, and Deferred Gratification in Children.* Doctoral dissertation, Washington University. *Dissertation Abstracts International,* 31:2275B (University Microfilms No. 70-18,918).
Claeys, W., & DeBoeck, P. (1976), The Influence of Some Parental Characteristics on Children's Primary Abilities and Field Independence: A Study of Adopted Children. *Child Development,* 47:842–845.
______ & Mandosi, M. (1977), Extended Family as an Environmental Correlate of the Test Performances of Eleventh Grade Zairese Subjects. In: *Basic Problems in Cross-Cultural Psychology: Selected Papers from the Third International Association for Cross-Cultural Psychology Held at Tilburg University, Tilburg, The Netherlands, July 12–16, 1976,* ed. Y. H. Poortinga. Amsterdam: Swets & Zeitlinger.
Clar, P. N. (1971), *The Relationship of Psychological Differentiation to Client Behavior in*

Vocational Choice Counseling. Doctoral dissertation, University of Michigan. *Dissertation Abstracts International,* 32:1837B (University Microfilms No. 71-23,723).

Coates, S. (1974), Sex Differences in Field Independence Among Preschool Children. In: *Sex Differences in Behavior,* ed. R. C. Friedman, R. M. Richart, & R. L. Vande Wiele. New York: Wiley, pp. 259–274.

——— (1975), Field Independence and Intellectual Functioning in Preschool Children. *Perceptual and Motor Skills,* 41:251–254.

——— Lord, M., & Jakabovics, E. (1975), Field Dependence-Independence, Social-Non-Social Play and Sex Differences in Preschool Children. *Perceptual and Motor Skills,* 40:195–202.

Coates, S. W. (1972), *Preschool Embedded Figures Test Manual.* Palo Alto, Calif.: Consulting Psychologists Press.

Constantinople, A. (1974), Analytical Ability and Perceived Similarity to Parents. *Psychological Reports,* 35:1335–1345.

Cooper, H. S. F., Jr. (1976a), A Reporter at Large: Life in a Space Station—1. *The New Yorker,* August 30, pp. 34–66.

——— (1976b), A Reporter at Large: Life in a Space Station—2. *The New Yorker,* September 6, pp. 34–70.

Cooper, L. W. (1967), *The Relationship of Empathy to Aspects of Cognitive Control.* Doctoral dissertation, Yale University. *Dissertation Abstracts,* 27:4549B–4550B (University Microfilms No. 67-7003).

Cooperman, E. W. (1976), *Cognitive Style and Social Reinforcement as Related to the Expectancy Effect.* Doctoral dissertation, St. John's University. *Dissertation Abstracts International,* 1977, 37:4113B (University Microfilms No. 77-1565).

Corah, N. L. (1965), Differentiation in Children and Their Parents. *Journal of Personality,* 33:300–308.

Cox, P. W., & Witkin, H. A. (1978), *Supplement No. 3, Field-Dependence-Independence and Psychological Differentiation: Bibliography with Index* (ETS RB 78-8). Princeton, N.J.: Educational Testing Service.

Crutchfield, R. S. (1957), Pesonal and Situational Factors in Conformity to Group Pressure. Paper presented at the Symposium, *Conflict, Decision and Post-Decision Phenomena* at the International Congress of Psychology, Brussels.

Cullen, J. F., Harper, C. R., & Kidera, G. J. (1969), Perceptual Style Differences Between Airline Pilots and Engineers. *Aerospace Medicine,* 4:407–408.

David, R. B. (1975), *Sensitivity of Body Cues and the Field Dependence-Independence Continuum.* Doctoral dissertation, Columbia University. *Dissertation Abstracts International,* 1976, 37:950B (University Microfilms No. 76-18,465).

Dawson, J. L. M. (1966), Kwashiorkor, Gynaecomastia, and Feminization Processes. *Journal of Tropical Medicine and Hygiene,* 69:175–179.

——— (1967a), Cultural and Physiological Influences upon Spatial-Perceptual Processes in West Africa—Part I. *International Journal of Psychology,* 2:115–128.

——— (1967b), Cultural and Physiological Influences upon Spatial-Perceptual Processes in West Africa—Part II. *International Journal of Psychology,* 2:171–185.

——— (1969), Theoretical and Research Bases of Bio-Social Psychology. *University of Hong Kong, Supplement to the Gazette,* 16:1–10.

——— (1970), Psychological Research in Hong Kong. *International Journal of Psychology,* 5:63–70.

——— (1972), Effects of Sex Hormones on Cognitive Style in Rats and Men. *Behavior Genetics,* 2:21–42.

——— Young, B. M., & Choi, P. P. C. (1974), Developmental Influences in Pictorial Depth Perception among Hong Kong Chinese Children. *Journal of Cross-Cultural Psychology,* 5:3–22.

DeFries, J. C., Ashton, G. C., Johnson, R. C., Kuse, A. R., McClearn, G. E., Mi, M. P., Rashad, M. N., Vandenberg, S. G., & Wilson, J. R. (1976), Parent-Offspring Resemblance for Specific Cognitive Abilities in Two Ethnic Groups. *Nature,* 261:131–133.

deGroot, J. C. (1968), *Emotional Climate of an Experimental Situation, Interaction Patterns, and Field Style of Subject.* Doctoral dissertation, University of Cincinnati. *Dissertation Abstracts International,* 1969, 30:843B–844B (University Microfilms No. 69-6333).

Dengerink, H. A., O'Leary, M. R., & Kasner, K. H. (1975), Individual Differences in Aggressive Responses to Attack: Internal-External Locus of Control and Field Dependence-Independence. *Journal of Research in Personality,* 9:191–199.

Dershowitz, Z. (1971), Jewish Subculture Patterns and Psychological Differentiation. *International Journal of Psychology,* 6:223–231.

DeWitt, G. W., & Averill, J. R. (1976), Lateral Eye Movements, Hypnotic Susceptibility and Field Independence-Dependence. *Perceptual and Motor Skills,* 43:1179–1184.

Diaz-Guerrero, R., & Holtzman, W. H. (1974), Learning by Televised "Plaza Sesamo" in Mexico. *Journal of Educational Psychology,* 66:632–643.

Dichgans, J., Held, R., Young, L. R., & Brandt, T. (1972), Moving Visual Scenes Influence the Apparent Direction of Gravity. *Science,* 178:1217–1219.

Dickie, K. E. (1969), *Effects of Compressing Visual Information and Field-Dependence on Acquiring a Procedural Skill.* Doctoral dissertation, Indiana University. *Dissertation Abstracts International,* 1970, 31:662A (University Microfilms No. 70-11,683).

Doebler, L. K. (1977), *A Study of the Effects of Teacher Awareness of the Educational Implications of Field-Dependent/Field-Independent Cognitive Style on Selected Classroom Variables.* Doctoral dissertation, University of Mississippi. *Dissertation Abstracts International,* 1978, 38:4040A (University Microfilms No. 77-28,957).

Doherty, M. A. (1968), *Relationship of the Global-Analytical and Open-Closed Dimensions Within and Between the Sexes in Cognitive Activity.* Unpublished doctoral dissertation, Loyola University of Chicago.

Dolecki, P. G. (1976), *The Effects of a Perceptual Training Program on Conservation Task Performance and Field Independence in First Grade Children.* Doctoral dissertation, Rutgers University. *Dissertation Abstracts International,* 37:878A (University Microfilms No. 76-17,311).

Dolson, M. A. (1973), *Hospitalization, Differentiation, and Dependency.* Doctoral dissertation, University of Pittsburgh. *Dissertation Abstracts International,* 1978, 34:2301B (University Microfilms No. 73-27,149).

Domash, L. G. (1973), *Selected Maternal Attitudes as Related to Sex, Sex-Role Preference and Level of Psychological Differentiation of the Five Year Old Child.* Doctoral dissertation, New York University. *Dissertation Abstracts International,* 34:2925B (University Microfilms No. 73-30,059).

Dowds, B. N., Fontana, A. F., Russakoff, L. M., & Harris, M. (1977), Cognitive Mediators Between Patients' Social Class and Therapists' Evaluations.

Archives of General Psychiatry, 34:917–920.

Dreyer, A. S. (1975), Family Interaction and Cognitive Style: Situation and Cross-Sex Effects. Paper delivered at the Symposium, *Beyond Father Absence: Conceptualization of Father Effects,* at the meeting of the Society for Research in Child Development, Denver, April.

——— Dreyer, C. A., & Nebelkopf, E. B. (1971), Portable Rod-and-Frame Test as a Measure of Cognitive Style in Kindergarten Children. *Perceptual and Motor Skills,* 33:775–781.

Dumsha, T. C., Minard, J., & McWilliams, J. (1973), Comparison of Two Self-Administered Field Dependency Measures. *Perceptual and Motor Skills,* 36:252–254.

Duncker, K. (1945), *On Problem-Solving.* Trans. L. S. Lees [*Psychological Monographs,* No. 270].

DuPreez, P. D. (1967), Field Dependence and Accuracy of Comparison of Time Intervals. *Perceptual and Motor Skills,* 24:467–472.

Duvall, N. S. (1969), *Field Articulation and the Repression-Sensitization Dimension in Perception and Memory.* Doctoral dissertation, University of North Carolina at Chapel Hill. *Dissertation Abstracts International,* 1970, 30:3864B (University Microfilms No. 70-3228).

Dyk, R. B. (1969), An Exploratory Study of Mother-Child Interaction in Infancy as Related to the Development of Differentiation. *Journal of the American Academy of Child Psychiatry,* 8:657–691.

——— & Witkin, H. A. (1965), Family Experiences Related to the Development of Differentiation in Children. *Child Development,* 30:21–55.

Ebenholtz, S. M., & Benzschawel, T. L. (1977), The Rod and Frame Effect and Induced Head Tilt as a Function of Observation Distance. *Perception & Psychophysics,* 22:491–496.

Eberhard, G., & Nilsson, L. (1967), The Rod-and-Frame Test and Emotional Maturity. *Acta Psychiatrica Scandinavica,* 43:39–51.

Eddy, S. (1974), *The Relationship of Field Articulation to Delay Capacity in Children.* Doctoral dissertation, Boston University. *Dissertation Abstracts International,* 35:2988B (University Microfilms No. 74-26,441).

Edgerton, N. E. (1975), *The Relationship of Cognitive Style of Young Children to Maternal Child-Rearing Practices.* Doctoral dissertation, Florida State University. *Dissertation Abstracts International,* 1976, 36:5135A (University Microfilms No. 76-2638).

Efland, A. D. (1965), *The Effect of Perceptual Training upon the Differentiation of Form in Children's Drawings.* Doctoral dissertation, Stanford University. *Dissertation Abstracts,* 1966, 26:3753 (University Microfilms No. 65-12,732).

Egeland, B., Wozniak, R., Schrimpf, V., Hage, J., Johnson, V., & Lederberg, A. (1976), Visual Information Processing: Evaluation of a Training Program for Children with Learning Disabilities. Paper presented at the meeting of the American Educational Research Association, San Francisco, April (ERIC Document Reproduction Service No. ED 132 161).

Eisner, D. A. (1971), *A Life Span Analysis of Perceptual Differentiation and Fixity-Mobility.* Doctoral dissertation, West Virginia University. *Dissertation Abstracts International,* 31:4968B–4969B (University Microfilms No. 71-4846).

Elliott, R., & McMichael, R. E. (1963), Effects of Specific Training on Frame Dependence. *Perceptual and Motor Skills,* 17:363–367.

English, H. B., & English, A. C. (1958), *A Comprehensive Dictionary of Psychological and Psychoanalytical Terms.* New York: David McKay.

Farley, F. H. (1974), Field Dependence and Approval Motivation. *Journal of General Psychology,* 91:153–154.

Feffer, M. (1959), The Cognitive Implications of Role-Taking Behavior. *Journal of Personality,* 27:152–168.

Feldman, C. F. (1971), Cognitive Development in Eskimos. Paper presented at the meeting of the Society for Research in Child Development, Minneapolis.

Finley, G. E., & Solla, J. (1975), Birth Order and Field Dependence-Independence: A Failure to Replicate. *Journal of Genetic Psychology,* 126:305–306.

______ ______ & Cowan, P. A. (1977), Field Dependence-Independence, Egocentrism, and Conservation in Young Children. *Journal of Genetic Psychology,* 131:155–156.

Fiscalini, J. A. (1974), *Field-Dependency with Social and Non-Social Stimuli.* Doctoral dissertation, Yeshiva University. *Dissertation Abstracts International,* 1975, 36:5638B (University Microfilms No. 75-9041).

Fleishman, E. A., Roberts, M. M., & Friedman, M. P. (1958), A Factor Analysis of Aptitude and Proficiency Measures in Radiotelegraphy. *Journal of Applied Psychology,* 42:127–137.

Forsius, H. (1973), The Finnish Skolt Lapp Children. *Acta Paediatrica Scandinavica Supplement,* 239:1–74.

Foss, D. S., Bever, T. G., & Silver, M. (1968), The Comprehension and Verification of Ambiguous Sentences. *Perception and Psychophysics,* 4:304–306.

Freedman, N., O'Hanlon, J., Oltman, P., & Witkin, H. A. (1972), The Imprint of Psychological Differentiation on Kinetic Behavior in Varying Communicative Contexts. *Journal of Abnormal Psychology,* 79:239–258.

Futterer, J. W. (1973), *Social Intelligence, Role-Taking Ability, and Cognitive Styles: A Factor Analytic Study.* Doctoral dissertation, Loyola University of Chicago. *Dissertation Abstracts International,* 34:1747B (University Microfilms No. 73-23,147).

Gaines, R. (1975), Developmental Perception and Cognitive Styles: From Young Children to Master Artists. *Perceptual and Motor Skills,* 40:983–998.

Gardner, R. W., Holzman, P. S., Klein, G. S., Linton, H. B., & Spence, D. P. (1959), *Cognitive Control: A Study of Individual Consistencies in Cognitive Behavior* [*Psychological Issues,* Monogr. 4]. New York: International Universities Press.

______ Jackson, D. N., & Messick, S. J. (1960), *Personality Organization in Cognitive Controls and Intellectual Abilities* [*Psychological Issues,* Monogr. 8]. New York: International Universities Press.

Geffen, L. F. (1971), *Relationships Between Visual Deficiencies and Cognitive Factors Before and After Tachistoscopic Training.* Doctoral dissertation, George Peabody College for Teachers. *Dissertation Abstracts International,* 32:1941A (University Microfilms No. 71-26,207).

Gill, N. T., Herdtner, T. J., & Lough, L. (1968), Perceptual and Socio-Economic Variables, Instruction in Body-Orientation, and Predicted Academic Success in Young Children. *Perceptual and Motor Skills,* 26:1175–1184.

Gillies, J., & Bauer, R. (1971), Cognitive Style and Perception of Success and Failure. *Perceptual and Motor Skills,* 33:839–842.

Glucksberg, S. (1956), *Perception and Problem-Solving.* Unpublished bachelor's thesis, City University of New York.

Goldstein, A. G., & Chance, J. E. (1965), Effects of Practice on Sex-Related Differences in Performance on Embedded Figures. *Psychonomic Science,* 3:361–362.

Goodenough, D. R. (1976), The Role of Individual Differences in Field Dependence as a Factor in Learning and Memory. *Psychological Bulletin,* 83:675–694.

——— Gandini, E., Olkin, I., Pizzamiglio, L., Thayer, D., & Witkin, H. A. (1977), A Study of X-Chromosome Linkage with Field Dependence and Spatial-Visualization. *Behavior Genetics,* 7:373–387.

——— & Karp, S. A. (1961), Field Dependence and Intellectual Functioning. *Journal of Abnormal and Social Psychology,* 63:243–246.

——— Sigman, E., Oltman, P. K., Rosso, J., & Mertz, H. (1979), Eye Torsion in Response to a Tilted Visual Stimulus. *Vision Research,* 19:1177–1179.

Goodman, D. R. (1971), *Cognitive Style Factors in Linguistic Performance with Ambiguous Sentences.* Unpublished master's thesis, York University, Canada.

Gordon, B. R. (1954), *An Experimental Study of Dependence-Independence in a Social and Laboratory Setting.* Unpublished doctoral dissertation, University of Southern California.

Gottschaldt, L. (1926), Über den Einfluss der Erfährung auf die Wahrnehmung von Figuren 1:Über den Einfluss Gehäufter Einprägung von Figuren auf Ihre Sichtbarkeit in Umfassenden Konfigurationen. *Psychol. Forsch.,* 8:261–317.

Gottschalk, L. A., & Gleser, G. C. (1969), *The Measurement of Psychological States Through the Context Analysis of Verbal Behavior.* Berkeley: University of California Press.

Gough, H. G., & Olton, R. M. (1972), Field Independence as Related to Nonverbal Measures of Perceptual Performance and Cognitive Ability. *Journal of Consulting and Clinical Psychology,* 38:338–342.

Graybiel, A., Kerr, W. A., & Bartley, S. H. (1948), Stimulus Thresholds of the Semicircular Canals as a Function of Angular Acceleration. *American Journal of Psychology,* 61:21–36.

Greenberg, G. G. (1960), *Visual Induction of Eye Torsion as Measured with an After-Image Technique, in Relation to Visual Perception of the Vertical.* Doctoral dissertation, Duke University. *Dissertation Abstracts,* 21:2382–2383 (University Microfilms No. 60-6028).

Greene, L. R. (1979), Psychological Differentiation and Social Structure. *Journal of Social Psychology,* 109:79–85.

Greene, M. A. (1972), *Client Perception of the Relationship as a Function of Worker-Client Cognitive Styles.* Doctoral dissertation, Columbia University. *Dissertation Abstracts International,* 33:3030A–3031A (University Microfilms No. 72-31,213).

Greenfield, N. L. (1969), *Field Independence-Dependence and Bargaining Behavior.* Unpublished master's thesis, Cornell University.

Grippin, P., Ohnmacht, F., & Clark, R. (1973), A Cross-Sectional Study of Cognitive Variables. Paper presented at the meeting of the Northeastern Educational Research Association, Ellenville, N.Y., November (ERIC Document Reproduction Service No. ED 095 997).

Gruenfeld, L. W., Weissenberg, P., & Loh, W. (1973), Achievement Values, Cognitive Style and Social Class: A Cross-Cultural Comparison of Peruvian and U.S. Students. *International Journal of Psychology,* 8:41–49.

Grunebaum, H., Weiss, J. L., Gallant, D., & Cohler, B. J. (1974), Attention in Young Children of Psychotic Mothers. *American Journal of Psychiatry,* 131:887–891.

Guetzkow, H. (1951), An Analysis of the Operation of Set in Problem-Solving Behavior. *Journal of General Psychology,* 45:219–244.

Guilford, J. P. (1967), *The Nature of Human Intelligence.* New York: McGraw-Hill.

Halverson, V. B. (1976), *Cognitive Styles of Preschool Seminole Indian Children.* Doctoral dissertation, Florida State University. *Dissertation Abstracts International,* 1977, 37:4198A–4199A (University Microfilms No. 76-29,446).

Haronian, F., & Sugerman, A. A. (1967), Fixed and Mobile Field Independence: Review of Studies Relevant to Werner's Dimension. *Psychological Reports,* 21:41–57.

Hartlage, L. C. (1970), Sex-Linked Inheritance of Spatial Ability. *Perceptual and Motor Skills,* 31:610.

Hauk, M. W. (1967), *Effects of Maternal Attitudes, Field-Dependence and Curiosity on Weight and Volume Conservation in Children.* Doctoral dissertation, Catholic University of America. *Dissertation Abstracts,* 28:2642B (University Microfilms No. 67-15,463).

Henn, V., Young, L. R., & Finley, C. (1974), Vestibular Nucleus Units in Alert Monkeys Are Also Influenced by Moving Visual Fields. *Brain Research,* 71:144–149.

Hoffman, D. A. (1975), *Cognitive Style and Intelligence: Their Relation to Leadership and Self Concept.* Doctoral dissertation, Ohio State University. *Dissertation Abstracts International,* 1976, 36:4133B (University Microfilms No. 76-3453).

Holtzman, W. H., Diaz-Guerrero, R., & Swartz, J. D. (1975), *Personality Development in Two Cultures: A Cross-Cultural Longitudinal Study of School Children in Mexico and the United States.* Austin, Texas: University of Texas Press.

Hoppe, C. M., Kagan, S. M., & Zahn, G. L. (1977), Conflict Resolution Among Field-Independent and Field-Dependent Anglo-American and Mexican-American Children and Their Mothers. *Developmental Psychology,* 13:591–598.

Horn, J. L. (1965), *Fluid and Crystallized Intelligence: A Factor Analytic Study of the Structure Among Primary Mental Abilities.* Doctoral dissertation, University of Illinois. *Dissertation Abstracts,* 26:479–480 (University Microfilms No. 65-7113).

——— (1973), Theory of Functions Represented among Auditory and Visual Test Performances. In: *Multivariate Analysis and Psychological Theory,* ed. J. R. Royce. New York: Academic Press, pp. 203–239.

——— & Cattell, R. B. (1966), Refinement and Test of the Theory of Fluid and Crystallized General Intelligence. *Journal of Educational Psychology,* 57:253–270.

——— & ——— (1967), Age Differences in Fluid and Crystallized Intelligence. *Acta Psychologica,* 26:107–129.

Hughes, P. C. (1973), *The Influence of the Visual Field upon the Visual Vertical in Relation to Ocular Torsion of the Eye.* Doctoral dissertation, University of Oklahoma. *Dissertation Abstracts International,* 33:4686B (University Microfilms No. 73-9158).

Hundleby, J. D., Pawlik, K., & Cattell, R. B. (1965), *Personality Factors in Objective Test Devices.* San Diego: R. R. Knapp.

Hurwitz, I., Wolff, P. H., Bortnick, B. D., & Kokas, K. (1975), Nonmusical Effects of the Kodaly Music Curriculum in Primary Grade Children. *Journal of Learning Disabilities,* 8:167–174.

Irving, D. D. (1970), *The Field-Dependence Hypothesis in Cross-Cultural Perspective.* Doctoral dissertation, Rice University. *Dissertation Abstracts International,* 31:3691B (University Microfilms No. 70-23,529).

Irwin, M., Klein, R. E., Engle, P. L., Yarbrough, C., & Nerlove, S. B. (1977), The Problem of Establishing Validity in Cross-Cultural Measurements. *Annals of the New York Academy of Sciences,* 285:308–325.

Johnston, P. K. (1974), *Relationship Between Perceptual Style, Achievement, and Childrearing Practices in Elementary-School Boys and Girls.* Doctoral dissertation, University of Southern California. *Dissertation Abstracts International,* 34:5169B–5170B (University Microfilms No. 74-9070).

Jones, P. A. (1975), Socialization Practices and the Development of Spatial Ability. In: *Readings in Cross-Cultural Psychology,* ed. J. L. M. Dawson & W. J. Lonner. Hong Kong: Hong Kong University Press, pp. 176–184.

Kagan, S. (1974), Field Dependence and Conformity of Rural Mexican and Urban Anglo-American Children. *Child Development,* 45:765–771.

______ & Zahn, G. L. (1975), Field Dependence and the School Achievement Gap Between Anglo-American and Mexican-American Children. *Journal of Educational Psychology,* 67:643–650.

______ ______ & Gealy, J. (1977), Competition and School-Achievement among Anglo-American Children. *Journal of Educational Psychology,* 69:432–441.

Kane, J. R. (1973), *Perceptual Differentiation in Ojibway and White Populations.* Unpublished bachelor's thesis, Queens University.

Karlin, J. E. (1942), The Factorial Isolation of the Primary Auditory Abilities. *Psychological Bulletin,* 39:453–454.

Karp, S. A. (1963), Field Dependence and Overcoming Embeddedness. *Journal of Consulting Psychology,* 27:294–302.

______ Kissin, B., & Hustmyer, F. E. (1970), Field Dependence as a Predictor of Alcoholic Therapy Dropouts. *Journal of Nervous and Mental Disease,* 150:77–83.

______ & Konstadt, N. (1971), The Children's Embedded Figures Test (CEFT). In: *Manual for the Embedded Figures Tests,* ed. H. A. Witkin, P. K. Oltman, E. Raskin, & S. A. Karp. Palo Alto, Calif.: Consulting Psychologists Press, pp. 21–26.

Katz, J. J., & Postal, P. M. (1964), *An Integrated Theory of Linguistic Descriptions.* Cambridge, Mass.: MIT Press.

Kirk, L., & Burton, M. (1977), Maternal Kinesic Behavior and Cognitive Development in the Child. *Annals of the New York Academy of Sciences,* 285:389–407.

Kirschenbaum, J. (1969), *Analytic-Global Cognitive Style and Concept Attainment Strategies.* Doctoral dissertation, Claremont Graduate School. *Dissertation Abstracts International,* 29:4868B–4869B (University Microfilms No. 68-18,276).

Klaiber, E. L., Broverman, D. M., & Kobayashi, Y. (1967), The Automatization Cognitive Style, Androgens, and Monoamine Oxidase. *Psychopharmacologia,* 11:320–336.

______ ______ Vogel, W., Abraham, G. E., & Cone, E. L. (1971), Effects of Infused Testosterone on Mental Performances and Serum LH. *Journal of Clinical Endocrinology and Metabolism,* 32:341–349.

Klebanoff, H. E. (1975), *Leadership: An Investigation of Its Distribution in Task-Oriented Small Groups.* Doctoral dissertation, Adelphi University. *Dissertation Abstracts International,* 1976, 36:3614B (University Microfilms No. 76-1420).

Klein, G. S., & Schlesinger, H. J. (1949), Where Is the Perceiver in Perceptual Theory? *Journal of Personality,* 18:32–47.

Klepper, I. L. (1969), Induction of Field-Dependence Changes by Body Attention Procedures. *Perceptual and Motor Skills,* 29:139–145.

Knobler, M. (1971), *Teacher's Guide to Project SEE.* Union, N.J.: Union Township Board of Education.

Koff, J. H. W. (1972), *Field Dependence and Psychotherapy Expectancies, Presenting Symptoms, Defensive Style, and Length of Stay in Psychotherapy.* Doctoral dissertation, George Washington University. *Dissertation Abstracts International,* 32:7312B (University Microfilms No. 72-18,590).

Kokas, K. (1969), Psychological Tests in Connection with Music Education in Hungary. *Journal of Research in Music Education,* 8:102–114.

Kolakowski, D., & Malina, R. M. (1974), Spatial Ability, Throwing Accuracy and Man's Hunting Heritage. *Nature,* October 4, pp. 410–412.

Komnenich, P., Lane, D. M., Dickey, R. P., & Stone, S. C. (1978), Gonadal Hormones and Cognitive Performance. *Physiological Psychology,* 6:115–120.

Kostlin-Gloger, G. (1974), *Sozialisation und Kognitive Stile.* Weinheim, Germany: Beltz.

Krippner, S., & Brown, D. P. (1973), Field Independence/Dependence and Electrosone 50 Induced Altered States of Consciousness. *Journal of Clinical Psychology,* 29:316–319.

Kugelmass, S., & Lieblich, A. (1975), *A Developmental Study of the Arab Child in Israel* (Scientific Report, Ford Foundation Grant 015.1261). Hebrew University, Human Development Center.

Kurtz, R. M. (1969), A Conceptual Investigation of Witkin's Notion of Perceptual Style. *Mind,* 78:522–533.

Laosa, L. M. (1976), Teaching Problem-Solving to Their Young Children: Strategies Used by Mexican-American and Anglo-American Mothers. Preliminary Analyses. Paper presented at the meeting of the Interamerican Congress of Psychology, Miami Beach, Florida, December.

Lawson, N. C. A. (1977), *Physical and Social Masculinity and Femininity in Relation to Sex-Typed Cognitive Abilities.* Doctoral dissertation, University of Texas at Austin. *Dissertation Abstracts International,* 1978, 38:6121B (University Microfilms No. 78-07338).

Lee, S. W. (1974), *Effects of Temporary Father-Absence and Parental Child Rearing Attitudes on the Development of Cognitive Abilities Among Elementary School Boys.* Doctoral dissertation, University of Texas at Austin. *Dissertation Abstracts International,* 35:483B (University Microfilms No. 74-14,728).

Lefever, M. M., & Ehri, L. C. (1976), The Relationship Between Field Independence and Sentence Disambiguation Ability. *Journal of Psycholinguistic Research,* 5:99–106.

Lega-Duguet, L. I. (1977), *A Cross-Cultural Study of the Relationship Between Field-Independence and Conservation.* Doctoral dissertation, Temple University. *Dissertation Abstracts International,* 1978, 38:5358A (University Microfilms No. 78-00579).

Leithwood, K. A., & Fowler, W. (1971), Complex Motor Learning in Four-Year-Olds. *Child Development,* 42:781–792.

Lester, D. (1976), The Relationship Between Some Dimensions of Personality. *Psychology,* 13:58–60.

Levy, J. (1969), Possible Basis for the Evolution of Lateral Specialization of the Human Brain. *Nature,* 224:614–615.

______ (1974), Psychobiological Implications of Bilateral Asymmetry. In: *Hemisphere Function in the Human Brain,* ed. S. J. Dimond & G. Beaumont. New York: Halsted Press, pp. 121–183.

Lichtenstein, J. H., & Saucer, R. T. (1974), Visual Dependency in the Erect and Supine Positions. *Journal of Applied Psychology,* 59:529–531.

Lifshitz, M. (1977), Person Perception and Social Interaction of Jewish and Druze Kindergarten Children in Israel. *Annals of the New York Academy of Sciences,* 285:338–354.

Linden, J. (1976), *Perception in Size-Invariance Situations as Related to Visual Aftereffect Perception and Rod-and-Frame-Test Performance* [*Psychological Research Bulletin,* 16:4]. Lund, Sweden: Lund University.

Linton, H. B. (1955), Dependence on External Influence: Correlates in Perception, Attitudes, and Judgment. *Journal of Abnormal and Social Psychology,* 51:502–507.

Loehlin, J. C., Sharan, S., & Jacoby, R. (1978), In Pursuit of the "Spatial Gene": A Family Study. *Behavior Genetics,* 8:27–41.

Lopez, L. C. (1976), *The Relationship Between Selected Cognitive Styles and Cooperation in a Prisoner's Dilemma Game Situation.* Doctoral dissertation, Ohio State University. *Dissertation Abstracts International,* 1977, 37:7043A–7044A (University Microfilms No. 77-10,565).

Louden, K. H. (1973), *Field Dependence in College Students as Related to Father Absence During the Latency Period.* Unpublished doctoral dissertation, Fuller Theological Seminary.

Lynn, D. B. (1962), Sex-Role and Parental Identification. *Child Development,* 33: 555–564.

——— (1969), Curvilinear Relation Between Cognitive Functioning and Distance of Child from Parent of the Same Sex. *Psychological Review,* 76:236–240.

MacArthur, R. S. (1970), Cognitive and Psychosocial Influences for Eastern Eskimos and Nsenga Africans: Some Preliminaries. Paper presented at the Memorial University of Newfoundland Symposium on Cross-Cultural Research, St. John's, October.

——— (1971), Mental Abilities and Psychosocial Environments: Igloolik Eskimos. Paper presented at the Mid-Project Review, International Biological Programme, Igloolik Project, Toronto, March.

——— (1973), Some Ability Patterns: Central Eskimos and Nsenga Africans. *International Journal of Psychology,* 8:239–247.

——— (1975), Differential Ability Patterns: Inuit, Nsenga, Canadian Whites. In: *Applied Cross-Cultural Psychology,* ed. J. W. Berry & W. J. Lonner. Amsterdam: Swets & Zeitlinger, pp. 237–241.

——— (1978), Ecology, Culture, and Cognitive Development: Canadian Native Youth. In: *The Canadian Ethnic Mosaic: A Quest for Identity,* ed. L. Driedger. Toronto: McClelland & Stewart, pp. 187–211.

Maccoby, E. E., & Jacklin, C. N. (1974), *The Psychology of Sex Differences.* Stanford, Calif.: Stanford University Press.

MacEachron, A. E., & Gruenfeld, L. W. (1978), The Effects of Family Authority Structure and Socioeconomic Status on Field Independence. *Journal of Social Psychology,* 104:49–56.

MacKay, D. G. (1966), To End Ambiguous Sentences. *Perception and Psychophysics,* 1:426–436.

——— & Bever, T. G. (1967), In Search of Ambiguity. *Perception and Psychophysics,* 2:193–200.

MacKinnon, A. A. (1972), Eskimo and Caucasian: A Discordant Note on Cognitive-Perceptual Abilities. In: *Proceedings of the 80th Annual Convention of the*

American Psychological Association, 7:303–304.

MacKinnon, D. W. (1962), The Personality Correlates of Creativity: A Study of American Architects. In: *Proceedings of the 14th International Congress of Applied Psychology. Vol. 2: Personality Research,* ed. G. Nielson. Copenhagen: Munksgaard, pp. 11–39.

Mahler, M. (1966), Notes on the Development of Basic Moods: The Depressive Affect. In: *Psychoanalysis—A General Psychology,* ed. R. M. Loewenstein, L. M. Newman, M. Schur, & A. J. Solnit. New York: International Universities Press, pp. 152–168.

______ Pine, F., & Bergman, A. (1975), *The Psychological Birth of the Human Infant.* New York: Basic Books.

Maloney, P. M. (1974), *Perceived Parental Child Rearing Patterns, Field Articulation, and Reading Achievement in Eighth Grade Girls.* Doctoral dissertation, Fordham University. *Dissertation Abstracts International,* 35:1503A (University Microfilms No. 74-19,704).

McCain, F. E. (1970), *The Effect of Figural and Verbal Task Demands During Observation Training on Field Articulation in Prospective Teachers.* Doctoral dissertation, Indiana University. *Dissertation Abstracts International,* 1971, 31:3964A (University Microfilms No. 70-23,370).

McCarrey, M. W. (1969), *Attitude Shift, Approval Need and Extent of Psychological Differentiation.* Unpublished doctoral dissertation, University of Ottawa.

McCarter, S. C. (1976), *A Description of Altered Visual Perceptual Differentiation as Affected by Instructional Procedures upon the Responses of Individuals to Visual Data.* Doctoral dissertation, North Texas State University. *Dissertation Abstracts International,* 37:3352A–3353A (University Microfilms No. 76-29,152).

McCarthy, R. J. (1967), *A Study of the Effect of Rail Walking on Improvement of Rod and Frame Performance of Alcoholics.* Unpublished master's thesis, University of Kansas.

McCord, M. M. (1973), *Comparative Effects of Selected Art Experiences upon Factors of Visual Perception.* Doctoral dissertation, Indiana University. *Dissertation Abstracts International,* 1974, 34:4880A–4881A (University Microfilms No. 74-2680).

McFie, J. (1961), The Effect of Education on African Performance on a Group of Intellectual Tests. *British Journal of Educational Psychology,* 31:232–240.

McGarvey, W. E. (1976), *Can Adjustment Cause Achievement?: A Cross-Lagged Panel Analysis* (Research Report 76-1). Los Angeles: University of Southern California, Social Science Research Institute, March.

McGee, M. G. (1978), Intrafamilial Correlations and Heritability Estimates for Spatial Ability in a Minnesota Sample. *Behavior Genetics,* 8:77–80.

McGilligan, R. P., & Barclay, A. G. (1974), Sex Differences and Spatial Ability Factors in Witkin's "Differentiation" Construct. *Journal of Clinical Psychology,* 30:528–532.

McGuire, L. S., Ryan, K. O., & Omenn, G. S. (1975), Congenital Adrenal Hyperplasia. II. Cognitive and Behavioral Studies. *Behavior Genetics,* 5:175–188.

McNett, C. W. (1970), A Settlement Pattern Scale of Cultural Complexity. In: *A Handbook of Method in Cultural Anthropology,* ed. R. Naroll & R. Cohen. New York: Natural History Press, pp. 872–886.

McWhinnie, H. J. (1967), The Effects of a Learning Experience upon the Preference for Complexity and Asymmetry in Fourth Grade Children. *California Journal of Educational Research,* 18:219–229.

______ (1968), The Effects of a Learning Experience upon the Preference for Complexity and Asymmetry in Fifth Grade Children. *California Journal of Educational Research,* 19:183–189.

______ (1970a), A Factor Analytic Study of Perceptual Behavior in 4th and 5th Grade Children. *Acta Psychologica,* 34:89–97.

______ (1970b), A Third Study of the Effects of a Learning Experience upon Preference for Complexity-Asymmetry in Fourth, Fifth, and Sixth Grade Children. *California Journal of Educational Research,* 21:216–225.

Mebane, D., & Johnson, D. L. (1970), A Comparison of the Performance of Mexican Boys and Girls on Witkin's Cognitive Tasks. *Interamerican Journal of Psychology,* 4:227–239.

Meek, F., & Skubie, V. (1971), Spatial Perception of Highly Skilled and Poorly Skilled Females. *Perceptual and Motor Skills,* 33:1309–1310.

Meizlik, F. (1973), *The Effect of Sex and Cultural Variables on Field Independence/Dependence in a Jewish Subculture.* Unpublished master's thesis, City University of New York.

Messer, S. B. (1976), Reflection-Impulsivity: A Review. *Psychological Bulletin,* 83: 1026–1052.

Messick, S., & French, J. W. (1975), Dimensions of Cognitive Closure. *Multivariate Behavioral Research,* 10:3–16.

Miller, L. B., & Dyer, J. L. (1975), *Four Preschool Programs: Their Dimensions and Effects* [*Monographs of the Society for Research in Child Development,* Vol. 40 (5–6, Serial No. 162)].

Minkowich, A. (1967), *Correlates of Ambivalence, Risk-Taking and Rigidity* (Final Scientific Report No. 3, Grant AF EOAR 65-32). European Office of Aerospace Research: United States Air Force, Air Force Office of Scientific Research.

Money, J. (1968), Cognitive Deficits in Turner's Syndrome. In: *Progress in Human Behavior Genetics,* ed. S. G. Vandenberg. Baltimore: Johns Hopkins, pp. 27–30.

______ & Alexander, D. (1966), Turner's Syndrome: Further Demonstration of the Presence of Specific Cognitional Deficiencies. *Journal of Medical Genetics,* 3:47–48.

Mooney, C. M., (1954), A Factorial Study of Closure. *Canadian Journal of Psychology,* 8:51–60.

Morelan, S. J., & Ortiz, F. I. (1975), The Effects of Personal and Impersonal Rewards on the Learning Performance of Field Independent-Dependent Mexican-American Children. *Colorado Journal of Educational Research,* 14:27–32.

Morgan, A. H. (1972), Hypnotizability and "Cognitive Styles": A Search for Relationships. *Journal of Personality,* 40:503–509.

Munroe, R. H., & Munroe, R. L. (1975), Infant Care and Childhood Performance in East Africa. Paper presented at the meeting of the Society for Research in Child Development, Denver, April (ERIC Document Reproduction Service No. ED 115 369).

Murdock, G. P. (1969), Correlations of Exploitative and Settlement Patterns. In: *Ecological Essays,* ed. D. Damas. National Museum of Canada Bulletin No. 230, Anthropological Series No. 86.

Naylor G. H. (1971), *Learning Styles at Six Years in Two Ethnic Groups in a Disadvantaged Area.* Doctoral dissertation, University of Southern California. *Dissertation Abstracts International,* 32:794A (University Microfilms No. 71-21,481).

Nebelkopf, E. B., & Dreyer, A. S. (1973), Continuous-Discontinuous Concept

Attainment as a Function of Individual Differences in Cognitive Style. *Perceptual and Motor Skills,* 36:655–662.

Nedd, A. N. B., & Gruenfeld, L. W. (1976), Field Dependence-Independence and Social Traditionalism: A Comparison of Ethnic Subcultures of Trinidad. *International Journal of Psychology,* 11:23–41.

_____ & Schwartz, H. (1977), A Cross-Cultural Investigation of the Relative Importance of Child Rearing and Socioeconomic Antecedents of Field-Dependence-Independence. *Journal of Psychology,* 96:63–70.

Nilsson, A., Almgren, P. E., Kohler, E. M., & Kohler, L. (1973), Enuresis: The Importance of Maternal Attitudes and Personality. *Acta Psychiatrica Scandinavica,* 49:114–130.

_____ Magnusson, P. A., & Vasko, T. (1972), *Reflexive Versus Perceptual Regulation: An Investigation of Nystagmus, Oculogyral Illusion, Motion-and-Median-Plane and Rod-and-Frame* [*Psychological Research Bulletin,* Vol. 12, No. 13]. Lund, Sweden: Lund University.

Nordquist, S. (1958), *The Perception of the Vertical Related to Selected Personality Characteristics.* Unpublished master's thesis, Texas Christian University.

Nyborg, H. (1976), *Sex Chromosome Abnormalities and Cognitive Performance. I: A Developmental Study of Cognitive Performance in Girls with Turner's Syndrome* [Psychological Reports Aarhus, Vol. 1, No. 2]. Risskov, Denmark: University of Aarhus, Institute of Psychology.

O'Connor, J. (1943), *Structural Visualization.* Boston: Human Engineering Laboratory.

Okonji, M. O., & Olagbaiye, O. O. (1975), Field Dependence and the Coordination of Perspectives. *Developmental Psychology,* 11:520.

Olesker, W. (1978), Cognition and the Separation-Individuation Process: A Study of Three Boys at Nursery School. *Psychoanalysis and Contemporary Thought,* 1:237–268.

Oliver, R. A. (1974), *Parental Influence on Children's Cognitive Style.* Doctoral dissertation, Iowa State University. *Dissertation Abstracts International,* 35:485B (University Microfilms No. 74-15,443).

Oltman, P. K., Goodenough, D. R., Witkin, H. A., Freedman, N., & Friedman, F. (1975), Psychological Differentiation as a Factor in Conflict Resolution. *Journal of Personality and Social Psychology,* 32:730–736.

Paclisanu, M. I. (1970), *Interacting Effects of Field Dependence, Stimulus Deprivation and Two Types of Reinforcement upon Problem-Solving in Elementary School Children.* Doctoral dissertation, Temple University. *Dissertation Abstracts International,* 31:2290B–2291B (University Microfilms No. 70-19,763).

Paeth, C. A. (1973), *A Likert Scaling of Student Value Statements, Field Independence-Field Dependence, and Experimentally Induced Change.* Doctoral dissertation, Oregon State University. *Dissertation Abstracts International,* 34:2288B–2289B (University Microfilms No. 73-25,368).

Palmer, R. D., & Field, P. B. (1971), Cognitive Factors in Hypnotic Susceptibility. *Journal of Consulting and Clinical Psychology,* 37:165.

Parente, J. A., & O'Malley, J. J. (1975), Training in Musical Rhythm and Field Dependence of Children. *Perceptual and Motor Skills,* 40:392–394.

Park, J., Johnson, R. C., DeFries, J. C., McClearn, G. E., Mi, M. P., Rashad, M. N., Vandenberg, S. G., & Wilson, J. R. (1978), Parent-Offspring Resemblance for Specific Cognitive Abilities in Korea. *Behavior Genetics,* 8:43–52.

Parlee, M. B. (1972), Comments on "Roles of Activation and Inhibition in Sex Differences in Cognitive Abilities" by D. M. Broverman, E. L. Klaiber, Y. Kobayashi, and W. Vogel. *Psychological Review,* 79:180–184.

Pascual-Leone, J. (1969), *Cognitive Development and Cognitive Style: A General Psychological Integration.* Unpublished doctoral dissertation, University of Geneva.

Paul, E. (1975), *A Study of the Relationship Between Separation and Field-Dependency in a Group of Three-Year-Old Nursery-School Children.* Unpublished master's thesis, Bank Street College of Education.

Pawlik, K. (1966), Concepts in Human Cognition and Aptitudes. In: *Handbook of Multivariate Experimental Psychology,* ed. R. B. Cattell. Chicago: Rand McNally, pp. 535-562.

Pearlstein, L. S. (1971), *The Relationships Between Intelligence and Cognitive Style and the Creative Ability of Kindergarten Age Children.* Unpublished master's thesis, University of Connecticut.

Pelto, P. J. (1968), The Differences Between "Tight" and "Loose" Societies. *Transaction,* April, 37–40.

Perez, P. P. (1958), *Experimental Instructions and Stimulus Content as Variables in the Size Constancy Perception of Schizophrenics and Normals.* Doctoral dissertation, New York University. *Dissertation Abstracts,* 18:2214–2215 (University Microfilms No. 24, 888).

Perkins, C. J. (1973), *A Study of Perceptual Correlates to Role-Taking Ability with Fourth Through Sixth Grade Children.* Doctoral dissertation, Oregon State University. *Dissertation Abstracts International,* 34:1261B–1262B (University Microfilms No. 73-21,319).

Petersen, A. C. (1976), Physical Androgyny and Cognitive Functioning in Adolescence. *Developmental Psychology,* 12:524–533.

Piaget, J., & Inhelder, B. (1956), *The Child's Conception of Space.* London: Routledge and Kegan Paul.

______ ______ (1962), *Le Developpement des Quantites Chez l'Enfant. Conservation et Atomisme.* Neuchatel & Paris: Delachaux & Niestle.

Pierson, J. S. (1965), *Cognitive Styles and Measured Vocational Interests of College Men.* Doctoral dissertation, University of Texas at Austin. *Dissertation Abstracts,* 26:875–876 (University Microfilms No. 65-8082).

Pizzamiglio, L. (1976), Field Dependence and Brain Organization. Paper presented at the Symposium, *Psychophysiological Studies of Field Dependence-Independence,* at the meeting of the American Psychological Association, Washington, D.C., September.

Podell, J. E., & Phillips, L. (1959), A Developmental Analysis of Cognition as Observed in Dimensions of Rorschach and Objective Test Performance. *Journal of Personality,* 27:439–463.

Pollack, I. W., & Kiev, A. (1963), Spatial Orientation and Psychotherapy: An Experimental Study of Perception. *Journal of Nervous and Mental Disease,* 137:93–97.

Powers, J. E., & Lis, D. J. (1977), Field Dependence-Independence and Performance with the Passive Transformation. *Perceptual and Motor Skills,* 45:759–765.

Preale, I., Amir Y., & Sharan, S. (1970), Perceptual Articulation and Task Effectiveness in Several Israel Subcultures. *Journal of Personality and Social Psychology,* 15:190–195.

Preston, C. E., (1964), Psychological Testing with Northwest Coast Alaskan

Eskimos. *Genetic Psychology Monographs,* 69:323–419.

Quinlan, D. M., & Blatt, S. J. (1972), Field Articulation and Performance under Stress: Differential Predictions in Surgical and Psychiatric Nursing Training. *Journal of Consulting and Clinical Psychology,* 39:517.

Raab, T. J. (1973), *An Experimental Study Exploring the Relationship Between Various Types of Reinforcement, Cognitive Style and Learning Among Sixth Grade Students.* Doctoral dissertation, Rutgers University. *Dissertation Abstracts International,* 1974, 34:3473B (University Microfilms No. 73-32,235).

Radin, J. H. (1961), *Authoritarianism in Relation to Perceptual Performance: The Relationship Between Degrees of Acceptance of Authoritarianism and Space Orientation.* Doctoral dissertation, New York University. *Dissertation Abstracts,* 1962, 22:4427–4428 (University Microfilms No. 62-1425).

Ramirez, M., & Price-Williams, D. (1974a), Cognitive Styles in Children: Two Mexican Communities. *Interamerican Journal of Psychology,* 8:93–101.

______ ______ (1974b), Cognitive Styles of Children of Three Ethnic Groups in the United States. *Journal of Cross-Cultural Psychology,* 5:212–219.

Rand, Y. (1975), *Dependance a l'Egard du Champ et Appartenance Culturelle* [*Monographies Francaises de Psychologie,* No. 28]. Paris: Centre National de la Recherche Scientifique.

Randolph, L. C. (1971), *A Study of the Effects of Praise, Criticism and Failure on the Problem Solving Performance of Field-Dependent and Field-Independent Individuals.* Doctoral dissertation, New York University. *Dissertation Abstracts International,* 32:3014B–3015B (University Microfilms No. 71-28,555).

Rapaczynski, W., Welkowitz, J., & Sadd, S. (1979), *Affect Judgment and Field Dependence.* (ETS RR 79-5). Princeton, N.J.: Educational Testing Service.

Rappoport, P. S. (1975), *The Effects of Field Dependence and High and Low Structured Human Potential Groups on Personal and Interpersonal Response.* Doctoral dissertation, Temple University. *Dissertation Abstracts International,* 36:3064B (University Microfilms No. 75-28,193).

Reeves, D. J. (1971), *The Assessment of Altered Differentiation as Affected by Experimental Treatments.* Doctoral dissertation, Illinois State University. *Dissertation Abstracts International,* 32:253A (University Microfilms No. 71-18,131).

Renzi, N. B. (1974), *A Study of Some Effects of Field Dependence-Independence and Feedback on Performance Achievement.* Doctoral dissertation, Hofstra University. *Dissertation Abstracts International,* 35:2059A (University Microfilms No. 74-21,861).

Ribback, B. H. B. (1957), *Factors Related to the Perceptual-Analytic Ability of Children.* Doctoral dissertation, Purdue University. *Dissertation Abstracts,* 18:302 (University Microfilms No. 24,396).

Roberts, M. J. R. (1964), *Attention and Cognitive Controls as Related to Individual Differences in Hypnotic Susceptibility.* Doctoral dissertation, Stanford University. *Dissertation Abstracts,* 25:4261 (University Microfilms No. 64-13,630).

Rohde, D. W. H. A. (1977), *A Study of Sex Differences and Interactions in Measures of Trust, Trusting Behavior, and Field Independence-Dependence.* Doctoral dissertation, University of Notre Dame. *Dissertation Abstracts International,* 38:2947B (University Microfilms No. 77-27,106).

Roodin, P. A., Broughton, A., & Vaught, G. M. (1974), Effects of Birth Order, Sex, and Family Size on Field Dependence and Locus of Control. *Perceptual and Motor Skills,* 39:671–676.

Rosenberg, E. S. (1975), *Some Psychological and Biological Relationships Between Masculinity and Femininity and Field Dependence and Field Independence.* Doctoral dissertation,

Northwestern University. *Dissertation Abstracts International,* 1976, 36:6453B (University Microfilms No. 76-13,106).

Rosner, S. (1956), *Studies of Group Pressure.* Unpublished doctoral dissertation, New School for Social Research.

Royce, J. R. (1973), The Conceptual Framework for a Multi-Factor Theory of Individuality. In: *Multivariate Analysis and Psychological Theory,* ed. J. R. Royce. London: Academic Press, pp. 305–407.

Russakoff, L. M., Fontana, A. F., Dowds, B. N., & Harris, M. (1976), Psychological Differentiation and Psychotherapy. *Journal of Nervous and Mental Disease,* 163:329–333.

St. John, J., Krichev, A., & Bauman, E. (1976), Northwestern Ontario Indian Children and the WISC. *Psychology in the Schools,* 13:407–411.

Salome, R. A., & Reeves, D. (1972), Two Pilot Investigations of Perceptual Training of Four- and Five-Year-Old Kindergarten Children. *Studies in Art Education,* 13:3–10.

Salomon, G. (1973), Cognitive Effects of Media: The Case of "Sesame Street" in Israel. Paper presented at the meeting of the International Society for the Study of Behavioral Development, Ann Arbor, Michigan, August.

Sanders, M., Scholz, J. P., & Kagan, S. (1976), Three Social Motives and Field Independence-Dependence in Anglo American and Mexican American Children. *Journal of Cross-Cultural Psychology,* 7:451–462.

Schaffer, M. C. (1969), *Parent-Child Similarity in Psychological Differentiation.* Doctoral dissertation, Purdue University. *Dissertation Abstracts International,* 30:1888B (University Microfilms No. 69-17,253).

Schooler, C. (1972), Childhood Family Structure and Adult Characteristics. *Sociometry,* 35:255–269.

Schubert, J., & Cropley, A. J. (1972), Verbal Regulation of Behavior and IQ in Canadian Indian and White Children. *Developmental Psychology,* 7:295–301.

Seder, J. A. (1957), *The Origin of Differences in Extent of Independence in Children: Developmental Factors in Perceptual Field Dependence.* Unpublished bachelor's thesis, Radcliffe College.

Serra, A., Pizzamiglio, L., Boari, A., & Spera, S. (submitted), *A Comparative Study of Cognitive Traits in Human Heterosomic Aneuploids and Sterile and Fertile Euploids.*

Shaffer, E. C. (1970), Field Articulation and Conformity. Paper presented at the meeting of the Southeastern Psychological Association, Louisville, Kentucky, April.

Shaffer, J. W. (1962), A Specific Cognitive Deficit Observed in Gonadal Aplasia (Turner's Syndrome). *Journal of Clinical Psychology,* 18:403–406.

Shapson, S. M. (1973), *Hypothesis Testing and Cognitive Style in Children.* Unpublished doctoral dissertation, York University.

Sherman, J. A. (1967), Problem of Sex Differences in Space Perception and Aspects of Intellectual Functioning. *Psychological Review,* 74:290–299.

——— (1971), *On the Psychology of Women: A Survey of Empirical Studies.* Springfield, Ill.: Thomas.

Sholtz, D. (1973), *The Development of Sex Differences in Field Independence.* Doctoral dissertation, Boston University. *Dissertation Abstracts International,* 33:6066B–6067B (University Microfilms No. 73-14,180).

Shulman, E. (1975), *Conformity in a Modified Asch-Type Situation.* Unpublished doctoral dissertation, City University of New York.

Sigman, E., Goodenough, D. R., & Flannagan, M. (1978), Subjective Estimates of Body Tilt and the Rod-and-Frame Test. *Perceptual and Motor Skills,* 47:1051–1056.

——— ——— ——— (1979), Instructions, Illusory Self-Tilt and the Rod-and-Frame Test. *Quarterly Journal of Experimental Psychology,* 31:155–165.

Singer, G., & Montgomery, R. B. (1969), Comment on Roles of Activation and Inhibition in Sex Differences in Cognitive Abilities. *Psychological Review,* 76:325–327.

Sinha, D. (1978), Perceptual Style Among Nomadic and Transitional Agriculturist Birhors. Paper presented at the Symposium, *Ecological Variables and Psychological Concepts,* at the Fourth International Congress, International Association for Cross-Cultural Psychology, Munich, August.

Soat, D. M. (1974), *Cognitive Style, Self-Concept, and Expressed Willingness to Help Others.* Doctoral dissertation, Marquette University. *Dissertation Abstracts International,* 35:2063A–2064A (University Microfilms No. 74-22,305).

Solar, D., Davenport, G., & Bruehl, D. (1969), Social Compliance as a Function of Field Dependence. *Perceptual and Motor Skills,* 29:299–306.

Spuhler, K. P. (1976), *Family Resemblance for Cognitive Performance: An Assessment of Genetic and Environmental Contributions to Variation.* Doctoral dissertation, University of Colorado. *Dissertation Abstracts International,* 37:1963B (University Microfilms No. 76-23,687).

Stafford, R. E. (1961), Sex Differences in Spatial Visualization as Evidence of Sex-Linked Inheritance. *Perceptual and Motor Skills,* 13:428.

Stanes, D., & Gordon, A. (1973), Relationships Between Conceptual Style Test and Children's Embedded Figures Test. *Journal of Personality,* 41:185–191.

Steingart, I., Freedman, N., Grand, S., & Buchwald, C. (1975), Personality Organization and Language Behavior: The Imprint of Psychological Differentiation on Language Behavior in Varying Communication Conditions. *Journal of Psycholinguistic Research,* 4:241–255.

Sutton-Smith, B., Baracca, F., Eadie, F., Mahony, D., & Zaren, S. (1977), A Developmental Psychology of Children's Film Making. Paper presented at the 1977 Conference on Culture and Communication, Temple University, Philadelphia, March.

Swan, G. A. (1973), *Machiavellianism, Impulsivity, Field Dependence-Independence, and Performance on the Prisoners' Dilemma Game.* Doctoral dissertation, Wayne State University. *Dissertation Abstracts International,* 1974, 34:5695B (University Microfilms No. 74-11,167).

Szeto, J. W. (1975), *The Effects of Search Practice and Perceptual Drawing Training upon Representational Drawing Performance and Visual Functions.* Doctoral dissertation, Illinois State University. *Dissertation Abstracts International,* 1976, 36:7135A (University Microfilms No. 76-9904).

Tannen, M. M. (1976), *A Comparative Study of Human Figure Drawings of Arab and Jewish Adolescents Based on the Koppitz and Marlens Analytic Schemes.* Unpublished master's thesis, City University of New York.

Tapia, L. L., San Roman, A., & Diaz-Guerrero, R. (1967), Percepcion, Inteligencia, Formacion de Conceptos y Cultura. In: *Aportaciones de la Psicologia a la Investigacion Transcultural,* ed. C. F. Hereford & L. Natalicio. Mexico City: Trillas, pp. 143–153.

Taylor, L. J., & Skanes, G. R. (1976), Cognitive Abilities in Inuit and White Children from Similar Environments. *Canadian Journal of Behavioural Science,* 8:1–8.

Templeton, W. B. (1973), The Role of Gravitational Cues in the Judgement of Visual Orientation. *Perception & Psychophysics,* 14:451–457.

Tendler, R. (1975), *Maternal Correlates of Differentiation in Hearing Children of the Deaf.* Doctoral dissertation, Yeshiva University. *Dissertation Abstracts International,* 1976, 36:4183B (University Microfilms No. 76-4563).

Throckmorton, R. S. (1974), *Role Playing, Social Dependence and Field Dependence: An Exploratory Study.* Doctoral dissertation, University of Nevada. *Dissertation Abstracts International,* 1975, 35:4712B (University Microfilms No. 75-5302).

Thurstone, L. L. (1944), *A Factorial Study of Perception.* Chicago: University of Chicago Press.

Tobacyk, J. J., Broughton, A., & Vaught, G. M. (1975), The Effects of Congruence-Incongruence Between Locus of Control and Field Dependence on Personality Functioning. *Journal of Consulting and Clinical Psychology,* 43:81–85.

Trent, E. R. (1974), *An Analysis of Sex Differences in Psychological Differentiation.* Doctoral dissertation, Ohio State University. *Dissertation Abstracts International,* 35:2416B (University Microfilms No. 74-24,414).

Tyler, L. E. (1965), *The Psychology of Human Differences,* 3rd Ed. New York: Appleton-Century-Crofts.

Van Leeuwen, M. S. (1978), A Cross-Cultural Examination of Psychological Differentiation in Males and Females. *International Journal of Psychology,* 13:87–122.

Vernon, P. E. (1965), Ability Factors and Environmental Influences. *American Psychologist,* 20:723–733.

——— (1972), The Distinctiveness of Field Independence. *Journal of Personality,* 40:366–391.

Waber, D. P. (1976), Sex Differences in Cognition: A Function of Maturation Rate? *Science,* 192:572–574.

——— (1977a), Biological Substrates of Field Dependence: Implications of the Sex Difference. *Psychological Bulletin,* 84:1076–1087.

——— (1977b), Sex Differences in Mental Abilities, Hemispheric Lateralization and Rate of Physical Growth at Adolescence. *Developmental Psychology,* 13:29–38.

Wachman, R. N. (1964), The Study of Social Influence: A Methodological Evaluation. *Bard Psychology Journal,* 3:3–25.

Wachtel, P. L. (1972), Field Dependence and Psychological Differentiation: Reexamination. *Perceptual and Motor Skills,* 35:179–189.

Wade, E. B. (1971), *Field-Independence, Authoritarianism, and Verbal Reinforcement in Anagram Solution.* Doctoral dissertation, Columbia University. *Dissertation Abstracts International,* 32:3625B–3626B (University Microfilms No. 72-1397).

Webb, D. (1972), *The Effect of Ordering and Contrast of Feedback and Perceptual Style on Liking of an Evaluative Source.* Doctoral dissertation, University of Cincinnati. *Dissertation Abstracts International,* 1973, 33:3966B (University Microfilms No. 73-3825).

Weinberg, H. J. (1970), *Changing Perceptions on the RFT by Conditioning Subjects to Relieve Dissonance and/or Escape from the Anxiety in a New Manner.* Doctoral dissertation, University of Nebraska. *Dissertation Abstracts International,* 31:1637A (University Microfilms No. 70-17,768).

Weiner, M. (1955), The Effects of Differently Structured Visual Fields on the Perception of Verticality. *American Journal of Psychology,* 68:291–293.

Weissman, H. J. (1971), *Sex Differences in Perceptual Style in Junior High School in Rela-*

tion to Nursery-School and Current Dependency and Sex Role Crystallization. Doctoral dissertation, Catholic University of America. *Dissertation Abstracts International,* 32:2390B (University Microfilms No. 71-25,551).

Weitz, J. M. (1971), *Cultural Change and Field Dependence in Two Native Canadian Linguistic Families.* Unpublished doctoral dissertation, University of Ottawa.

Weller, L., & Sharan, S. (1971), Articulation of the Body Concept Among First-Grade Israeli Children. *Child Development,* 42:1553–1559.

Wendt, R. A., & Burwell, E. (1964), Test Performance of Jewish Day-School Students. *Journal of Genetic Psychology,* 105:99–103.

Werner, H. (1948), *Comparative Psychology of Mental Development,* Rev. Ed. Chicago: Follett.

______ (1957), The Concept of Development from a Comparative and Organismic Point of View. In: *The Concept of Development: An Issue in the Study of Human Behavior,* ed. D. B. Harris. Minneapolis: University of Minnesota Press.

White, B. W. (1954), Visual and Auditory Closure. *Journal of Experimental Psychology,* 48:234–240.

Wilkie, D. M. (1973), Attention and "Visual Field Dependency" in the Pigeon. *Journal of Experimental Analysis of Behavior,* 20:7–15.

Willemsen, E., Buchholz, A., Budrow, M. S., & Geannacopulos, N. (1973), Relationship Between Witkin's Rod-and-Frame Task and Piaget's Water-Line Task for College Women. *Perceptual and Motor Skills,* 36:958.

Winestine, M. C. (1969), Twinship and Psychological Differentiation. *Journal of the American Academy of Child Psychiatry,* 8:436–455.

Witkin, H. A. (1948), *The Effect of Training and of Structural Aids on Performance in Three Tests of Space Orientation.* Washington, D.C.: Civil Aeronautics Administration, Division of Research.

______ (1949), *Perception of Body Position and of the Position of the Visual Field.* [*Psychological Monographs,* No. 302].

______ (1950a), Individual Differences in Ease of Perception of Embedded Figures. *Journal of Personality,* 19:1–15.

______ (1950b), Perception of the Upright when the Direction of the Force Acting on the Body Is Changed. *Journal of Experimental Psychology,* 40:93–106.

______ (1952), Further Studies of Perception of the Upright When the Direction of the Force Acting on the Body Is Changed. *Journal of Experimental Psychology,* 43:9–20.

______ (1964), Origins of Cognitive Style. In: *Cognition: Theory, Research, Promise,* ed. C. Scheerer. New York: Harper and Row, pp. 172–205.

______ (1965), Psychological Differentiation and Forms of Pathology. *Journal of Abnormal Psychology,* 70:317–336.

______ (1978), *Cognitive Styles in Personal and Cultural Adaptation. The 1977 Heinz Werner Lectures.* Worcester, Mass.: Clark University Press.

______ & Asch, S. E. (1948a), Studies in Space Orientation. III. Perception of the Upright in the Absence of a Visual Field. *Journal of Experimental Psychology,* 38:603–614.

______ ______ (1948b), Studies in Space Orientation. IV. Further Experiments on Perception of the Upright with Displaced Visual Fields. *Journal of Experimental Psychology,* 38:762–782.

______ & Berry, J. W. (1975), Psychological Differentiation in Cross-Cultural Perspective. *Journal of Cross-Cultural Psychology,* 6:4–87.

______ Cox, P. W., & Friedman, F. (1976), *Supplement No. 2, Field-Dependence-*

Independence and Psychological Differentiation: Bibliography with Index (ETS RB 76-28). Princeton, N.J.: Educational Testing Service.

—— —— —— Hrishikesan, A. G., & Siegel, K. N. (1974), *Supplement No. 1, Field-Dependence-Independence and Psychological Differentiation: Bibliography with Index* (ETS RB 74-42). Princeton, N.J.: Educational Testing Service.

—— Dyk, R. B., Faterson, H. F., Goodenough, D. R., & Karp, S. A. (1962), *Psychological Differentiation.* New York: Wiley. (Reprinted: Potomac, Md.: Erlbaum, 1974.)

—— & Goodenough, D. R. (1977), Field Dependence and Interpersonal Behavior. *Psychological Bulletin,* 84:661–689.

—— —— & Karp, S. A. (1967), Stability of Cognitive Style from Childhood to Young Adulthood. *Journal of Personality and Social Psychology,* 7:291–300.

—— —— & Oltman, P. K. (1979), Psychological Differentiation: Current Status. *Journal of Personality and Social Psychology,* 37:1127–1145.

—— Lewis, H. B., Hertzman, M., Machover, K., Meissner, P. B., & Wapner, S. (1954), *Personality Through Perception.* New York: Harper. (Reprinted: Westport, Conn.: Greenwood Press, 1972.)

—— —— & Weil, E. (1968), Affective Reactions and Patient-Therapist Interactions Among More Differentiated and Less Differentiated Patients Early in Therapy. *Journal of Nervous and Mental Disease,* 146:193–208.

—— Moore, C. A., Goodenough, D. R., & Cox, P. W. (1977), Field-Dependent and Field-Independent Cognitive Styles and Their Educational Implications. *Review of Educational Research,* 47:1–64.

—— —— Oltman, P. K., Goodenough, D. R., Friedman, F., & Owen, D. (1976), *A Longitudinal Study of the Role of Cognitive Styles in Academic Evolution During the College Years.* Graduate Record Examinations Board Research Report 76-10R. Princeton, N.J.: Educational Testing Service.

—— —— —— —— —— —— & Raskin, E. (1977), The Role of the Field-Dependent and Field-Independent Cognitive Styles in Academic Evolution: A Longitudinal Study. *Journal of Educational Psychology,* 69:197–211.

—— Oltman, P. K., Chase, J. B., & Friedman, F. (1971), Cognitive Patterning in the Blind. In: *Cognitive Studies. Vol. 2: Deficits in Cognition,* ed. J. Hellmuth. New York: Brunner/Mazel, pp. 16–46.

—— —— Cox, P. W., Ehrlichman, E., Hamm, R. M., & Ringler, R. W. (1973), *Field-Dependence-Independence and Psychological Differentiation: A Bibliography Through 1972 with Index* (ETS RB 73-62). Princeton, N.J.: Educational Testing Service.

—— Price-Williams, D., Bertini, M., Christiansen, B., Oltman, P. K., Ramirez, M., & van Meel, J. (1974), Social Conformity and Psychological Differentiation. *International Journal of Psychology,* 9:11–29.

Wober, M. (1966), Sensotypes. *Journal of Social Psychology,* 70:181–189.

—— (1967), Adapting Witkin's Field Independence Theory to Accommodate Information from Africa. *British Journal of Psychology,* 58:29–38.

Wohlford, P., & Liberman, D. (1970), Effect of Father Absence on Personal Time, Field Independence, and Anxiety. *Proceedings of the 78th Annual Convention of the American Psychological Association,* 5:263–264.

Wolitzky, D. L. (1973), Cognitive Controls and Person Perception. *Perceptual and Motor Skills,* 36:619–623.

Woodworth, R. S. (1938), *Experimental Psychology.* New York: Holt.

Wu, J. J. (1967), *Cognitive Style and Task Performance—A Study of Student Teachers.* Doctoral dissertation, University of Minnesota. *Dissertation Abstracts,* 1968, 29:176A (University Microfilms No. 68-7408).

Yalom, I. D., Green, R., & Fisk, N. (1973), Prenatal Exposure to Female Hormones: Effect on Psychosexual Development in Boys. *Archives of General Psychiatry,* 28:554–561.

Yen, W. M. (1973), *Sex-Linked Major-Gene Influences on Human Spatial Abilities.* Doctoral dissertation, University of California, Berkeley. *Dissertation Abstracts International,* 1974, 34:5667B (University Microfilms No. 74-8856).

Zadik, B. (1968), [Field Dependence-Independence Among Oriental and Western School Children.] *Megamot,* 16:51–58.

NAME INDEX

Abad, M., 91
Abelew, T., 83
Abraham, G. E., 69
Adevai, G., 91
Adler, R., 39
Alexander, D., 73
Almgren, P. E., 88
Amir, Y., 91
Annis, R. C., 96
Antler, L., 39
Asch, S. E., 7, 14
Ashton, G. C., 74
Austrian, R. W., 42
Averill, J. R., 39

Bacon, M. K., 94
Balance, W. D. G., 39
Ball, S., 78
Banta, T. J., 78
Baracca, F., 78
Baraga, E. S., 40
Baran, S., 83, 96
Barclay, A. G., 27, 87
Barrett, G. V., 37, 38
Barry, H., 94
Bartley, S. H., 37
Bauer, R., 39
Bauman, E., 96
Beckerle, G. P., 39
Bell, D. R., 84
Bennett, M., 96
Benzschawel, T. L., 35
Bercovici, A. M., 84
Bergman, A., 40
Bergman, H., 25, 27, 36
Berland, J. C., 91
Berry, J. W., vii, 52, 83, 87, 89, 90, 91, 92, 94, 95, 96, 97, 98
Bertini, M., 88, 91
Bever, T. G., 32, 33
Bieri, J., 88
Biller, H. B., 88
Birmingham, D. L., 39
Blake, R. R., 2
Blatt, S. J., 44, 59
Bloomberg, M., 63
Boari, A., 73
Bock, R. D., 74
Bogatz, G. A., 78
Bortnick, B. D., 64, 78, 79
Botkin, E. B., 63
Brandsma, J. M., 39
Brandt, T., 34
Brinkman, E. H., 77
Britain, S. D., 91
Brooks, I. R., 91, 96
Brosgole, L., 35
Broughton, A., 48
Broverman, D. M., 68, 69, 70, 71
Broverman, I. K., 68, 69, 70, 71
Brown, D. P., 39
Bruehl, D., 39

Bruner, J. S., 2
Bruner, P. B., 83
Buchholz, A., 26
Buchwald, C., 42
Budrow, M. S., 26
Burton, M., 85
Burwell, E., 91
Busch, J. C., 39
Busse, T. V., 28, 83, 84, 85, 87

Cabe, P. A., 37
Campbell, J. T., 91
Carter, S. L., 74, 75
Cattell, R. B., 29, 30, 32, 48, 49
Cavalli-Sforza, L., 100
Cegalis, J. A., 48
Chance, J. E., 77
Chandra, S., 96
Chapman, J. W., 91
Chase, J. B., 77
Child, I. L., 94
Choi, P. P. C., 83
Chomsky, N., 32
Christiansen, B., 88, 91
Churchill, R. D., 77
Clack, G. S., 67
Claeys, W., 83, 88
Clar, P. N., 45
Clark, R., 26
Coates, S. W., 66, 67
Cohler, B. J., 74
Cone, E. L., 69
Constantinople, A., 88
Coombs, C. H., 77
Cooper, H. S. F., Jr., 37
Cooper, L. W., 46
Cooperman, E. W., 39
Corah, N. L., 74
Cowan, P. A., 28
Cox, P. W., 4, 16, 42, 59, 78
Cristal, R. M., 35
Crooks, L. A., 91
Cropley, A. J., 96
Crutchfield, R. S., 39
Cullen, J. F., 38
Curtis, J. M., 77
Cusumano, D. R., 87

Davenport, G., 39
David, R. B., 80
Davis, J. K., vii
Dawson, J. L. M., 72, 73, 83, 88, 89, 95, 96, 98
DeBoeck, P., 83
DeFries, J. C., 74
deGroot, J. C., 42
Dengerink, H. A., 84
DeRidder, L. M., 39
Dershowitz, Z., 88, 91
DeWitt, G. W., 39
Diaz-Guerrero, R., 78, 88, 91
Dichgans, J., 34
Dickie, K. E., 67
Dickie, R. P., 70
Doebler, L. K., 38
Doherty, M. A., 67
Dolecki, P. G., 64, 78, 79
Dolson, M. A., 39
Domash, L. G., 83
Dowds, B. N., 41
Dreyer, A. S., 29, 66, 67, 85, 88
Dreyer, C. A., 66, 67
Dumsha, T. C., 25
Duncker, K., 26, 63
DuPreez, P. D., 48
Duvall, N. S., 84
Dyer, J. L., 78
Dyk, R. B., 3, 17, 18, 19, 20, 25, 27, 65, 66, 81, 82, 84, 86

Eadie, F., 78
Ebenholtz, S. M., 35
Eberhard, G., 39
Eddy, S., 67
Edgerton, N. E., 83
Efland, A. D., 78
Egeland, B., 78
Ehri, L. C., 33
Ehrlichman, E., 4
Eisner, D. A., 26, 36
Eliot, T. S., 4
Elliott, R., 77, 80
Emmerich, W., vii
Engelbrekston, K., 25, 27, 36
Engle, P. L., 39
English, A. C., 57
English, H. B., 57

Farley, F. H., 39
Faterson, H. F., 3, 17, 18, 19, 20, 25, 27, 65, 66, 81, 82, 84

Feffer, M., 46
Feldman, C. F., 96
Feldman, M. W., 100
Field, P. B., 39
Finley, C., 34
Finley, G. E., 28, 67
Fiscalini, J. A., 46
Fisk, N., 73
Flannagan, M., 35
Fleishman, E. A., 30
Fontana, A. F., 41, 42
Forsius, H., 96
Foss, D. S., 32
Fowler, W., 78, 80
Freedman, N., 42, 45
French, J. W., 27, 31
Friedman, F., 4, 45, 59, 77, 78
Friedman, M. P., 30
Futterer, J. W., 46

Gaines, R., 77
Gallant, D., 74
Gandini, E., 75
Gardner, R. W., 2, 27
Gealy, J., 39
Geannacopulos, N., 26
Geffen, L. F., 78
Gervasi, A., 39
Gill, N. T., 80
Gillies, J., 39
Gleser, G. C., 42
Glucksberg, S., 17, 26
Goldstein, A. G., 77
Goodenough, D. R., x, 3, 4, 16, 17, 18, 19, 20, 25, 27, 28, 35, 36, 38, 39, 42, 44, 45, 48, 51, 57, 59, 61, 65, 66, 67, 68, 76, 77, 78, 81, 82, 84, 89
Goodman, D. R., 33
Gordon, A., 67
Gordon, B. R., 39
Gottschaldt, L., 77
Gottschalk, L. A., 42
Gough, H. G., 26, 27
Grand, S., 42
Graybiel, A., 37
Green, R., 73
Greenberg, G. G., 35
Greene, L. R., 42
Greene, M. A., 43
Greenfield, N. L., 84
Grippin, P., 26
Gruenfeld, L. W., 67, 87, 91
Grunebaum, H., 74
Guetzkow, H., 28
Guilford, J. P., 25

Hage, J., 78
Halverson, V. B., 91
Hamm, R. M., 4
Haronian, F., 63
Harper, C. R., 38
Harrell, T. W., 77
Harris, M., 17, 27, 41, 42
Hartlage, L. C., 74
Hauk, M. W., 83
Held, R., 34
Henn, V., 34
Herdtner, T. J., 80
Hertzman, M., 2, 11, 12, 15, 18, 21, 65
Hoffman, D. A., 39
Holtzman, W. H., 78, 89
Holzer, B., 39
Holzman, P. S., 2
Hoppe, C. M., 86
Horn, J. L., 29, 30
Hrishikesan, A. G., 4
Hughes, P. C., 35
Hundleby, J. D., 48, 49
Hurwitz, I., 64, 78, 79
Hustmyer, F. E., 43

Inhelder, B., 26, 28
Irvine, S., vii
Irving, D. D., 83
Irwin, M., 39

Jacklin, C. N., 30, 66
Jackson, D. N., 2, 27
Jacoby, R., 74, 75
Jakabovics, E., 66
Johnson, D. L., 83
Johnson, R. C., 74
Johnson, V., 78
Johnston, P. K., 85
Jones, P. A., 83, 96

Kagan, S. M., 39, 86, 91
Kane, J. R., 96
Karlin, J. E., 30
Karp, S. A., 3, 17, 18, 19, 20, 25, 27, 36,

43, 57, 61, 65, 66, 67, 68, 81, 82, 84
Kasner, K. H., 84
Katz, J. J., 32
Kerr, W. A., 37
Kidera, G. J., 38
Kiev, A., 46
Kirk, L., 85
Kirschenbaum, J., 29
Kissin, B., 43
Klaiber, E. L., 68, 69, 70, 71
Klebanoff, H. E., 39
Klein, G. S., 1, 2, 3
Klein, R. E., 39
Klepper, I. L., 77
Knobler, M., 79
Kobayashi, Y., 68, 69, 70
Koff, J. H. W., 41
Kohler, E. M., 88
Kohler, L., 88
Kokas, K., 64, 78, 79
Kolakowski, D., 74, 75, 98
Komnenich, P., 70
Konstadt, N., 67
Kostlin-Gloger, G., 83
Krech, D., 2
Krichev, A., 96
Krippner, S., 39
Kugelmass, S., 91
Kurtz, R. M., 57
Kuse, A. R., 74

Lane, D. M., 70
Laosa, L. M., 85
Lawson, N. C. A., 70, 71, 72
Lederberg, A., 78
Lee, S. W., 83, 87, 89
Leen, D., 48
Lefever, M. M., 33
Lega-Duguet, L. I., 91
Leithwood, K. A., 78, 80
Lester, D., 48
Levy, J., 51
Lewis, H. B., 2, 11, 12, 15, 18, 21, 42, 43, 65
Liberman, D., 87
Lichtenstein, J. H., 35, 38
Lieblich, A., 91
Lifshitz, M., 91
Linden, J., 25
Linton, H. B., 2, 39
Lis, D. J., 33
Loehlin, J. C., 74, 75
Loh, W., 91
Lopez, L. C., 39
Lord, M., 66
Louden, K. H., 87
Lough, L., 80
Lynn, D. B., 87

MacArthur, R. S., 83, 96
Maccoby, E. E., 30, 66
MacEachron, A. E., 87
Machover, K., 2, 11, 12, 15, 18, 21, 65
MacKay, D. G., 32, 33
MacKinnon, A. A., 96
MacKinnon, D. W., 45
Magnusson, P. A., 37
Mahler, M., 40
Mahoney, M. H., 91
Mahony, D., 78
Malina, R. M., 98
Maloney, P. M., 83
Mandosi, M., 88
McCain, F. E., 78
McCarrey, M. W., 39
McCarter, S. C., 78
McCarthy, R. J., 80
McClearn, G. E., 74
McCord, M. M., 78
McFie, J., 96
McGarvey, W. E., 91
McGee, M. G., 74, 75, 77
McGilligan, R. P., 27
McGough, W. E., 91
McGuire, L. S., 73
McManis, D. L., 84
McMichael, R. E., 77, 80
McNett, C. W., 94
McWhinnie, H. J., 25, 36, 78, 80
McWilliams, J., 25
Mebane, D., 83
Meek, F., 80
Meissner, P. B., 2, 11, 12, 15, 18, 21, 65
Meizlik, F., 88
Mertz, H., 35
Messer, S. B., 48
Messick, S. J., vii, 2, 27, 31
Mi, M. P., 74

Miller, L. B., 78
Minard, J., 25
Minkowich, A., 88
Money, J., 73
Montgomery, R. B., 69
Mooney, C. M., 31
Moore, C. A., 16, 42, 59, 77
Morelan, S. J., 39
Morgan, A. H., 39
Munroe, R. H., 86
Munroe, R. L., 86
Murdock, G. P., 93

Naylor, G. H., 91
Nebelkopf, E. B., 29, 66, 67
Nedd, A. N. B., 67, 83
Nerlove, S. B., 39
Nicholls, J. G., 91
Nilsson, A., 37, 88
Nilsson, L., 39
Nordquist, S., 39
Nyborg, H., 73

O'Connor, J., 74
O'Hanlon, J., 42
Ohnmacht, F., 26
Okonji, M. O., 28
Olagbaiye, O. O., 28
O'Leary, M. R., 84
Olesker, W., 40
Oliver, R. A., 74
Olkin, I., 75
Oltman, P. K., vii, 4, 20, 35, 42, 45, 48, 51, 59, 77, 78, 88, 89, 91
Olton, R. M., 26, 27
O'Malley, J. J., 78, 80
Omenn, G. S., 73
Ortiz, F. I., 39
Owen, D., 59, 77, 78

Paclisanu, M. I., 39
Paeth, C. A., 39
Palmer, R. D., 39, 68, 69, 70, 71
Parente, J. A., 78, 80
Park, J., 74
Parlee, M. B., 69
Pascual-Leone, J., vii, 26, 27, 36
Paul, E., 40
Pawlik, K., 29, 48, 49
Pearlstein, L. S., 67
Pelto, P. J., 89
Perez, P. P., 27
Perkins, C. J., 46
Petersen, A. C., 71, 72, 75
Phillips, L., 31
Piaget, J., 26, 28
Pierson, J. S., 45
Pine, F., 40
Pizzamiglio, L., 25, 73, 75
Podell, J. E., 31
Pollack, I. W., 46
Poortinga, Y. H., vii
Postal, P. M., 32
Powers, J. E., 33
Preale, I., 91
Preston, C. E., 96
Price-Williams, D., 83, 88, 91

Quinlan, D. M., 44, 59

Raab, T. J., 39
Radin, J. H., 91
Ramirez, M., 83, 88, 91
Ramsey, G. V., 2
Rand, Y., 91
Randolph, L. C., 84
Rapaczynski, W., 46
Rappoport, P. S., 42
Rashad, M. N., 74
Raskin, E., 59, 77
Reeves, D. J., 78
Renzi, N. B., 67
Ribback, B. H. B., 83
Ringler, R. W., 4
Roberts, M. J. R., 39
Roberts, M. M., 30
Rock, D. A., 91
Rohde, D. W. H. A., 39
Roodin, P. A., 48
Rosenberg, E. S., 70, 71
Rosner, S., 39
Rosso, J., 35
Royce, J. R., vii, 29, 49
Russakoff, L. M., 41, 42
Ryan, K. O., 73

Sadd, S., 46
St. John, J., 96
Salome, R. A., 78
Salomon, G., 78

Sanders, M., 91
San Roman, A., 89
Saucer, R. T., 35, 38
Schaffer, M. C., 39, 74
Schlesinger, H. J., 1, 3
Scholz, J. P., 91
Schooler, C., 87, 88
Schrimpf, V., 78
Schubert, J., 96
Schwartz, H., 83
Seder, J. A., 83, 84
Serra, A., 73
Shaffer, E. C., 73
Shaffer, J. W., 73
Shapson, S. M., 29, 48
Sharan, S., 74, 75, 91
Sherman, J. A., 30
Sholtz, D., 74, 85
Shulman, E., 39, 45
Siegel, K. N., 4
Sigman, E., 35
Silver, M., 32
Silverman, A. J., 91
Singer, G., 69
Sinha, D., 96
Skanes, G. R., 96
Skubie, V., 80
Soat, D. M., 39
Solar, D., 39
Solla, J., 28, 67
Spence, D. P., 2
Spera, S., 73
Spuhler, K. P., 74, 83
Stafford, R. E., 74
Stanes, D., 67
Steingart, I., 42
Stone, S. C., 70
Sugerman, A. A., 63
Sutton-Smith, B., 78
Swan, G. A., 39
Swartz, J. D., 88, 89
Szeto, J. W., 78

Tannen, M. M., 91
Tapia, L. L., 89
Taylor, L. J., 96
Templeton, W. B., 35
Tendler, R., 83
Thayer, D., 75
Thornton, C. L., 37, 38
Throckmorton, R. S., 39
Thurstone, L. L., 25
Tobacyk, J. J., 48
Trent, E. R., 77, 87, 88
Tyler, L. E., 66

Vandenberg, S. G., 74
Van Leeuwen, M. S., 87, 91, 94, 97, 98, 100
van Meel, J., 88, 91
Vasko, T., 37
Vaught, G. M., 48
Vernon, P. E., 29, 32, 36, 83
Vogel, W., 68, 69, 70, 71

Waber, D. P., 69, 71, 72, 73
Wachman, R. N., 39
Wachtel, P. L., 58
Wade, E. B., 84
Wapner, S., 2, 11, 12, 15, 18, 21, 65
Warburton, F. W., 48, 49
Webb, D., 39
Wechsler, 61
Weil, E., 42, 43
Weinberg, H. J., 39
Weiner, M., 77
Weiss, J. L., 74
Weissenberg, P., 91
Weissman, H. J., 39
Weitz, J. M., 96
Welkowitz, J., 46
Weller, L., 91
Wendt, R. A., 91
Werner, H., 26, 63, 100
White, B. W., 30
Wilkie, D. M., 77
Willemsen, E., 26
Wilson, J. R., 74
Winestine, M. C., 40
Witkin, H. A., ix, x, 2, 3, 4, 7, 11, 12, 13, 14, 15, 16, 17, 18, 19, 20, 21, 25, 27, 38, 39, 42, 43, 44, 45, 48, 51, 52, 57, 59, 65, 66, 67, 68, 76, 77, 78, 81, 82, 88, 89, 90, 91, 92, 95, 97, 98
Wober, M., 96
Wohlford, P., 87
Wolff, P. H., 64, 78, 79
Wolitzky, D. L., 46
Woodworth, R. S., 29
Wozniak, R., 78

Wu, J. J., 46

Yalom, I. D., 73
Yarbrough, C., 39
Yen, W. M., 75
Young, B. M., 83
Young, L. R., 34

Zadik, B., 91
Zahn, G. L., 39, 86, 91
Zaren, S., 78

SUBJECT INDEX

Activity-passivity in field approach, 17; *see also* Restructuring
Adaptation
role of field dependence-independence in, 44, 50, 59, 63, 65, 95, 97, 98, 99, 100–101
role of perception in, 1, 2, 3
see also Ecological-cultural adaptation
Adrenogenital syndrome, 73
Africa, 83, 85, 86, 88, 90, 96
Age changes, 65–68, 100
interpersonal relations and skills and, 66
perception of the upright and, 65
restructuring and, 65–66
sex differences and, 66–68
Aggression and hostility, expression of, 82, 84
Analytical ability; *see* Articulated-global field approach; Disembedding; Field dependence-independence; Restructuring
Analytical-perceptual training, 78–79
Analytical triad; *see* Perceptual-organization factor
Articulated-global field approach, 15, 17–18, 20, 22, 23, 24, 47, 57, 58
defined, 18
see also Restructuring ability
Articulation of body concept, 20, 90
definition, current, 90
see also Figure Drawing Test
Art training, 77–78
Athletic training, 80
Attention-concentration factor, 61
Australian Arunta, 96
Automatization, 3, 68, 69
Autonomy of external referents, 34, 38–43, 47–56, 58, 60, 95
cognitive restructuring skills and, 49–52, 54, 55, 60
interpersonal competencies and, 43–47, 49–50, 54, 55–56, 60
in perception, 34, 38, 39, 43, 48, 49
in social behavior, 20, 21, 22, 38–43, 48–49, 55–56, 66, 81, 101
see also Child-rearing practices and socialization, training for autonomy; Field dependence-independence; Perception of the upright; Self-nonself segregation; Sense of separate identity; Social-interpersonal relations, autonomy in

Berzins Psychotherapy Expectancy Inventory, 41
Biological factors in development; *see* Genetic factors; Hormonal factors
Bipolar-neutral nature of field dependence-independence concept, 14, 37, 38, 59, 60, 63, 99

Block Design test, 61, 73, 90
Body-adjustment test (BAT), 8, 9, 10, 13, 14, 34, 35, 36, 38, 41, 42, 53, 58, 60, 61, 66, 80, 82, 90
  described, 9–10
  modification of performance on, 13
  processes involved in, 34–35, 36, 38
  sex differences and, 66
Body concept; *see* Articulation of body concept
Brain lateralization; *see* Differentiation, hemispheric

Canada, 96
Child-rearing practices and socialization, 52, 81–89, 90, 91, 92, 94, 96, 97, 98, 99, 100, 101
  conformity, emphasis on, 52, 82, 84, 89–91, 92, 94
  cultural differences and, 52, 87, 88, 89–92, 94, 96–97, 98, 99, 100, 101
  father's influence, 86–89, 90
  mother's influence, 86–89, 90
  parent-child interaction, observed, 84–6
  sex-role modeling, 87–89, 94
  training for autonomy, 52, 81–84, 88–89, 90, 91, 94, 99, 101
Children's Embedded Figures Test (CEFT), 67
Chinese, Hong Kong, 83, 96
Closure flexibility; *see* Flexibility of closure
Closure speed; *see* Speed of closure
Cognitive restructuring; *see* Restructuring ability
Cognitive style(s), 1, 2, 4–5, 56–61, 61–62, 68, 98
  ability and, 57, 58, 60, 61–62
  characteristics of, 57, 58, 59, 60
  definition, 57
  field dependence-independence as example of, 56–61
  historical origins of concept, 1, 2
  intelligence and, 61–62
  see also individual styles by name
Columbia, 91
Concept attainment; *see* Learning, discrimination
Conceptualizing style, 3
Conflict resolution, 45, 86
Conformity; *see* Child-rearing practices and socialization; Cultural differences, social conformity
Conservation, 26, 27, 79
Constancy, perceptual, 25, 27
Constricted-flexible control, 2
Controls; *see* Defenses and controls
Convergent production of figural transformations, 25
Critical exactness factor, 49
Critical practicality factor, 49
Cross-cultural comparisons; *see* Cultural differences
Cuba, 91
Cultural differences, 52, 59, 87, 89–101
  ecological demands and, 92–97, 98, 99–100, 101
  field dependence-independence, development of, and, 52, 89–92, 94–97, 98, 99, 101
  sex differences and, 87, 91–92, 94, 97, 98, 100
  social conformity, stress on, 89, 90–91, 92, 94
  social structure, 90, 91, 92, 94, 97, 99
Cultural evolution, 92–93, 97–101

Decentration, 26
Defenses and controls, 18, 20, 21–22
Dependency, 39; *see also* Autonomy of external referents
Differentiation, 3–4, 18–22, 24, 51–52, 56, 80, 81–82
  characteristics of, 18, 19, 20
  development and, 18–19, 20
  field dependence-independence as expression of, 3, 18–19, 22
  hemispheric, 19, 20, 51–52, 69, 71–72, 73–74
  indicators of, 19–20
  integration and, 20–21
  interrelations among indicators, 20
  pathology and, 21–22
  self-object; *see* Self-nonself segregation; Sense of separate identity; Social-interpersonal relations, autonomy in, separation-individuation

Disembedding
in intellectual functioning and problem solving, 17
in perception, 14–17, 24–25, 34, 35, 36, 37, 38, 43, 45, 46, 47, 53, 55, 61, 66–67, 68, 70, 71, 72, 73, 74, 75, 77, 78, 80, 83, 84–85, 86, 87
restructuring ability and, 17–18, 27–30, 35
in verbal domain, 31–32, 55
see also Embedded-figures test(s); Restructuring ability
Druze, 91
Duncker problems, 26

Ecological-cultural adaptation, 92–101
cultural evolution; field dependence-independence and, 92–93, 97–101
hunting and farming societies, comparison of, 59, 92–97, 98, 99–101; field dependence-independence and, 59, 92, 94–97, 99–101
Education, level of, 96
Educational implications; *see* Mobility-fixity; Training
Ego psychology, 1–2
Einstellung problems, 28
Embedded-figures test(s), 15, 16, 17, 24–25, 26, 27–30, 33, 34, 36, 39, 40, 41, 42, 43, 44, 45, 46, 47, 53, 60, 61, 67, 73, 74, 76, 77, 78, 79, 80, 82, 83, 84, 85, 90
Children's EFT, 67, 83
described, 15, 16
modification of performance on, 77
Preschool EFT, 67
restructuring ability, relation to, 27–30
sex differences and, 67
see also Disembedding
Endocrine functioning; *see* Hormonal factors in development
Environmental factors in development; *see* Child-rearing and socialization practices; Cultural differences; Ecological-cultural adaptation; Training
Equivalence range, 2
Eskimo, 83, 90, 96

Extraversion-introversion, 48
Eye torsion, 35, 53

Factor-analytic dimensions, 25, 29, 30, 31, 36, 48–49, 53–54, 60, 61
Father's role in development, 86–89, 90
Feffer's egocentrism task, 46
Field dependence-independence
adaptive role of, 44, 50, 59, 63, 65, 95, 97, 98, 99, 100–101
bipolar-neutral nature, 14, 37, 38, 59, 60, 63, 99
as cognitive style, 2–3, 56–61
defined as degree of autonomy from external referents, 49–56, 58; *see also* Autonomy of external referents
defined as overcoming embedding contexts, 14–15, 22, 34, 35–36, 37, 38, 47, 56; *see also* Disembedding
defined as reliance on gravitational vs. visual cues in perception of the upright, 8–14, 34–38, 47, 56, 58; *see also* Perception of the upright
as expression of psychological differentiation, 3, 18–19, 22
history and development of the concept, 7–18, 34, 56–57, 58
measurement, 60; *see also* Body-adjustment test; Embedded-figures test(s); Rod-and-frame test; Rotating-room test
modification of; cue salience, 13–14; training, 63–64, 77–81
origins and development of, 52, 60, 65–101
cultural evolution and, 92–93, 97–101
group differences in, 52, 89–97; cultural influences, 52, 59, 87, 89–101; ecological factors, 92–101
individual differences in, 60, 66, 68–89, 100; age changes, 65–68, 100; child-rearing, 52, 81–89, 90, 91, 92, 94, 96, 97, 98, 99, 100, 101; genetic factors, 74–76, 98–99, 100; hormonal effects, 68–74, 98; training, 63–64, 77–81, 96, 101
as perceptual component of articulated-vs.-global field approach, 15, 17–18, 22, 47, 57

reasons for research interest, 3
restructuring ability and, 23–27, 35–36, 38, 47, 49–56, 58–59, 60, 62, 79–80
disembedding, 24–25; functional fixity, 26; perceptual constancy, 25; perspectivism, 26–27, representation of the horizontal coordinate, 26; speed of closure, 25–26
stability of, 68
theory and model, revisited, 47–64
Figi, 96
Figure-drawing test, 21, 90; *see also* Articulation of body concept
Flexibility of closure, 25, 29, 30, 31, 36, 49, 57; *see also* Disembedding
Functional fixity, 26, 27

Genetic factors, 74–76, 98–99, 100
Greenland, 96

Heredity; *see* Genetic factors
Holland, 91
Hormonal factors in development, 68–74, 98
perception of the upright and, 71
restructuring ability and, 68–74

Illusion of movement
oculogyral, 37
self, 35, 36, 37–38, 53
Independence vs. subduedness factor, 49
India, 96
Indians, Canadian, 96
Indians, Native American, 91
Intellectual functioning and problem solving, 17, 26, 28, 46, 52, 57, 61
Intelligence, 29, 30, 61–62, 73
Israel, 91
Italy, 91

Jews, 91

Kwashiorkor, 73

Labrador, 96
Laterality; *see* Differentiation, hemispheric

Learning, discrimination, 28–29, 48, 78
Learning style, 28–29, 48
Leveling-sharpening, 2
Locus of control, 48

Masculinity-femininity; *see* Hormonal factors in development
Matching Familiar Figures Test (MFFT), 48
Maturation rate, physical
restructuring ability and, 69, 71, 72
see also Physical-sexual characteristics
Mexican Americans, 85, 91
Mexico, 83, 91
Mobility-fixity, 62–64, 81
Modeling; *see* Sex-role modeling
Mother's role in development, 86–89, 90
Music training, 77–78, 79

Newfoundland, 96
New Look movement, 1, 2, 3
New Zealand, 91

Occupation and vocational interests, 38, 44–46, 59, 77–78

Pakistan, 91
Parent-child interaction, 84–86; *see also* Child-rearing practices and socialization; Social-interpersonal relations, autonomy in, separation-individuation
Pathology, 21–22, 82
Perception
adaptive role of, 1, 2, 3
individual differences in, 2, 7, 8–9, 13, 14–15, 17, 18, 19, 34, 35, 38, 53
New Look movement, 1, 2, 3
personality and, 1, 2, 3, 48–49
see also Disembedding; Field dependence-independence; Perception of the upright; Restructuring ability
Perception of the upright, 7–14, 15, 17, 34–38, 39, 43, 45, 46, 47, 48, 50, 52, 53, 54, 55, 56, 58, 60, 65, 77, 79–80

astronauts and, 37–38
factor-analytic studies and, 36, 53, 54, 60
field dependence-independence and, 8–14, 34–38, 47, 56, 58
modification of performance, 13–14, 77
processes involved in, 34–38
restructuring ability and, 23, 24–27, 35–36, 38, 47, 53, 54, 55, 79–80
self-consistency across situations, 7, 13
tests of; *see* Body-Adjustment test; Rod-and-frame Test; Rotating-room test
see also Field dependence-independence
Perceptual constancy; *see* Constancy, perceptual
Perceptual-organization factor, 61, 90
Personality, 1, 2, 3, 18, 21–22, 39, 44, 48–49
Person perception, 46
Perspectivism, 26–28, 55
social, 46
see also Spatial-visualization ability
Peru, 91
Physical-sexual characteristics
restructuring ability and, 70, 71
see also Maturation rate, physical
Preschool Embedded Figures Test (PEFT), 67
Problem solving; *see* Intellectual functioning and problem solving
Project SEE, 79
Promethean will vs. subduedness factor; *see* Independence vs. subduedness factor
Psychological differentiation; *see* Differentiation

Reflection-impulsivity, 3, 48
Reinforcement, 84
Representation of the horizontal coordinate, 26, 27
Restructuring ability, 17–18, 23–34, 35–36, 38, 47, 49–56, 59, 60, 61, 62, 65–67, 68, 69, 70, 71, 72, 73, 76, 77, 78, 79–81, 83, 84, 89, 90, 92, 95, 96, 97, 99, 101
in auditory domain, 30, 51, 53–54
autonomy of external referents and, 49–52, 54, 55, 60
brain lateralization and, 51–52
defined, 51
development of, 51, 60, 66
interpersonal competencies and, 45–47, 49–50, 54, 62
perception of the upright, relation to, 23, 24–27, 35–36, 38, 47, 49, 53, 54, 55, 79–80
relation among visual-spatial dimensions, 27–30, 53, 61
relation of visual-spatial dimensions to other restructuring dimensions, 30–34, 53–54
in social domain, 45–47
in verbal domain, 31–34, 52, 53–54
in visual-spatial domain, 23–34, 35–56, 38, 47, 51, 52, 53, 61
see also Conservation; Disembedding; Functional fixity; Perceptual constancy; Perspectivism; Representation of the horizontal coordinate; Speed of closure
Rod-and-frame test (RFT), 8, 9, 11, 13, 14, 25, 26, 34, 35, 36, 37, 38, 39, 41, 42, 44, 46, 53, 58, 60, 61, 66, 67, 68, 71, 72, 73, 76, 77, 80, 82, 85, 90, 96
described, 9, 11
modification of performance on, 77
processes involved in 34, 35, 36, 37, 38, 53
sex differences and, 66, 67, 72
supine, 35, 38
Rorschach test, 21
Rotating-room test (RRT), 8, 9, 12, 13, 14, 58
described, 9, 12–13

Self-nonself segregation, 18, 19, 50, 51, 77, 81–82, 86, 87, 89, 92, 100
child-rearing practices and, 81–82, 86, 87, 92
field dependence-independence and, 50–51, 81–82, 89, 92
see also Sense of separate identity; Social interpersonal relations, autonomy in
Self-reliance; *see* Autonomy of external referents

Sense of separate identity, 20, 21–22 *see also* Self-nonself segregation; Social-interpersonal relations, autonomy in
Separation-individuation model, 40
Sesame Street, 78
Set-breaking, 28
Sex differences, 30, 66–68, 72, 86–89, 91–92, 94, 97, 98, 100
  age and, 66–68
  cultural differences and, 87, 91–92, 94, 97, 98, 100
  in disembedding, 66–67, 72
  in perception of the upright, 66, 67–68, 72
  in restructuring skills, 66, 72
  sex-role modeling and, 86–89
  in social-interpersonal skills, 66
  in spatial-visualization ability, 30
Sex-linked recessive model; *see* Genetic factors
Sex-role modeling, 74, 87–89
Skylab space program, 37–38
Social-interpersonal relations, autonomy in, 20, 21, 22, 38–43, 48–49, 52, 55–56, 66, 81, 101
  ambiguity in social situations, effects of, 39, 41–43, 48
  opinion formation, 39
  separation-individuation, 40–41, 81, 83, 84, 88–89, 99
  structure, need for in therapy, 41–43
  see also Autonomy of external referents; Child-rearing practices and socialization, training for autonomy; Self-nonself segregation; Sense of separate identity
Social-interpersonal skills, 43–47, 49–50, 54, 56, 58, 60, 62, 66, 81, 90, 95, 99
  autonomy and, 49–50, 54
  cognitive restructuring and, 45–47, 49–50, 54, 62
  development of, 50, 60, 66
Socialization; *see* Child-rearing practices and socialization
Social structure, tight vs. loose, 90, 91, 92, 94, 97
Social training, 55–56, 64, 81; *see also* Child-rearing practices and socialization
Spatial orientation; *see* Perception of the upright; Spatial-visualization ability
Spatial-visualization ability, 25, 29–30, 36, 51–52, 66, 67, 70, 71, 72, 73, 74, 75–76, 77, 80, 98
  defined, 29
  embedded-figures test, relation, to, 27–28
  as a factor-analytic dimension, 29, 30
  field dependence-independence and, 30
  perception of the upright, relation to, 26–27
  sex differences in, 30
  see also Perspectivism
Speed of closure, 25–26, 27, 29, 30, 31, 36, 49
  embedded-figures test, relation to, 27
  perception of the upright, relation to, 25–26
Structuring; *see* Restructuring ability

Tavistock Institute of Human Relations model, 42
Thematic Apperception Test (TAT), 21, 82
Therapy, 41–43, 46, 55–56
Three-mountain problem, 28
Tolerance for unrealistic experiences, 2
Training, 63–64, 77–81, 96, 101
  art and music, 77–78, 79
  athletic, 80
  direct, 77
  perceptual-analytical, 78–79
  social, 55–56, 64, 81
  transfer of; as test for new model of field dependence-independence, 55, 77–81
Trinidad, 83
Turner's syndrome, 73
Twins and twinning reaction, 40–41

U.I. 19 temperament factor, 49

Value judgments in field dependence-independence concept; *see* Bipolar-neutral nature of field dependence-independence concept
Verbal skills, 31–34, 51–52, 55, 61–62, 73

grammatical transformation, 33–34
sentence disambiguation, 32–33, 34, 55
verbal comprehension, 61–62
verbal disembedding, 31–32, 55
Vestibular system, role of, in perception of upright, 8, 34, 35, 36–37, 47
Vocational interests; *see* Occupation and vocational interests

Water-level problem, 26; *see also* Representation of the horizontal coordinate
Wechsler intelligence scales, factor analysis of subtests, 61
West India, 83
Williams Expectancy Inventory, 41

X-linked genetic model; *see* Genetic factors

ABOUT THE AUTHORS

HERMAN A. WITKIN received a Ph.D. from New York University in 1939. He taught at Brooklyn College from 1940 to 1952, and was a Professor in the Department of Psychiatry of the State University of New York Downstate Medical Center from 1952 to 1971. In 1971 he joined the staff of Educational Testing Service, where he served as Distinguished Research Scientist and Chairman of the Personality and Social Behavior Research Group until his death in July of 1979.

DONALD R. GOODENOUGH received a B.A. from Stanford University in 1950 and a Ph.D. from the University of Rochester in 1955. He held appointments as Assistant Professor, Associate Professor, and Professor during his tenure in the Department of Psychiatry of the State University of New York Downstate Medical Center from 1954 to 1971. He has been a Senior Research Psychologist at Educational Testing Service since 1971.

PSYCHOLOGICAL ISSUES

No. 1—ERIK H. ERIKSON: *Identity and the Life Cycle: Selected Papers.* Historical Introduction by David Rapaport

No. 2—I. H. PAUL: *Studies in Remembering: The Reproduction of Connected and Extended Verbal Material*

No. 3—FRITZ HEIDER: *On Perception, Event Structure, and Psychological Environment: Selected Papers.* Preface by George S. Klein

No. 4—RILEY W. GARDNER, PHILIP S. HOLZMAN, GEORGE S. KLEIN, HARRIET LINTON, and DONALD P. SPENCE: *Cognitive Control: A Study of Individual Consistencies in Cognitive Behavior*

No. 5—PETER H. WOLFF: *The Developmental Psychologies of Jean Piaget and Psychoanalysis*

No. 6—DAVID RAPAPORT: *The Structure of Psychoanalytic Theory: A Systematizing Attempt*

No. 7—OTTO PÖTZL, RUDOLF ALLERS, and JAKOB TELER: *Preconscious Stimulation in Dreams, Associations, and Images: Classical Studies.* Introduction by Charles Fisher

No. 8—RILEY W. GARDNER, DOUGLAS N. JACKSON, and SAMUEL J. MESSICK: *Personality Organization in Cognitive Controls and Intellectual Abilities*

No. 9—FRED SCHWARTZ and RICHARD O. ROUSE: *The Activation and Recovery of Associations*

No. 10—MERTON M. GILL: *Topography and Systems in Psychoanalytic Theory*

No. 11—ROBERT W. WHITE: *Ego and Reality in Psychoanalytic Theory: A Proposal Regarding the Independent Ego Energies*

No. 12—IVO KOHLER: *The Formation and Transformation of the Perceptual World.* Introduction by James J. Gibson

No. 13—DAVID SHAKOW and DAVID RAPAPORT: *The Influence of Freud on American Psychology*

No. 14—HEINZ HARTMANN, ERNST KRIS, and RUDOLPH M. LOEWENSTEIN: *Papers on Psychoanalytic Psychology*

No. 15—WOLFGANG LEDERER: *Dragons, Delinquents, and Destiny: An Essay on*

Positive Superego Functions. Introduction by Roy Schafer

No. 16—PETER AMACHER: *Freud's Neurological Education and Its Influence on Psychoanalytic Theory*

No. 17—PETER H. WOLFF: *The Causes, Controls, and Organization of Behavior in the Neonate*

No. 18/19—ROBERT R. HOLT, Ed.: *Motives and Thought: Psychoanalytic Essays in Honor of David Rapaport*

No. 20—JOHN CHYNOWETH BURNHAM: *Psychoanalysis and American Medicine, 1894–1918: Medicine, Science, and Culture*

No. 21—HELEN D. SARGENT, LEONARD HORWITZ, ROBERT S. WALLERSTEIN, and ANN APPELBAUM: *Prediction in Psychotherapy Research: A Method for the Transformation of Clinical Judgments into Testable Hypotheses*

No. 22—MARJORIE GRENE, Ed.: *Toward a Unity of Knowledge*

No. 23—FRED SCHWARTZ and PETER H. SCHILLER: *A Psychoanalytic Model of Attention and Learning*

No. 24—BERNARD LANDIS: *Ego Boundaries*

No. 25/26—EMANUEL PETERFREUND in collaboration with JACOB T. SCHWARTZ: *Information, Systems, and Psychoanalysis: An Evolutionary Biological Approach to Psychoanalytic Theory*

No. 27—LOUIS BREGER, IAN HUNTER, and RON W. LANE: *The Effect of Stress on Dreams*

No. 28—EDITH LEVITOV GARDUK and ERNEST A. HAGGARD: *Immediate Effects on Patients of Psychoanalytic Interpretations*

No. 29—ERICH GOLDMEIER: *Similarity in Visually Perceived Forms.* Foreword by Irvin Rock

No. 30—MARTIN MAYMAN, Ed.: *Psychoanalytic Research: Three Approaches to the Experimental Study of Subliminal Processes*

No. 31—NANETTE HEIMAN and JOAN GRANT, Eds.: *Else Frenkel-Brunswik: Selected Papers*

No. 32—FRED SCHWARTZ, Ed.: *Scientific Thought and Social Reality: Essays by Michael Polanyi*

No. 33—STANLEY I. GREENSPAN: *A Consideration of Some Learning Variables in the Context of Psychoanalytic Theory: Toward a Psychoanalytic Learning Perspective*

No. 34/35—JOHN E. GEDO and GEORGE H. POLLOCK, Eds.: *Freud: The Fusion of Science and Humanism: The Intellectual History of Psychoanalysis*

No. 36—MERTON M. GILL and PHILIP S. HOLZMAN, Eds.: *Psychology versus Metapsychology: Psychoanalytic Essays in Memory of George S. Klein*

No. 37—ROBERT N. EMDE, THEODORE J. GAENSBAUER, and ROBERT J. HARMON: *Emotional Expression in Infancy: A Biobehavioral Study*

No. 38—DAVID SHAKOW: *Schizophrenia: Selected Papers*

No. 39—PAUL E. STEPANSKY: *A History of Aggression in Freud.* Foreword by Roy Schafer

No. 40—Joseph de Rivera: *A Structural Theory of the Emotions.* Introductory Essay by Hartvig Dahl

No. 41—Hannah S. Decker: *Freud in Germany: Revolution and Reaction in Science, 1893–1907*

No. 42/43—Allan D. Rosenblatt and James T. Thickstun: *Modern Psychoanalytic Concepts in a General Psychology*—Parts 1 & 2

No. 44—Herbert J. Schlesinger, Ed.: *Symbol and Neurosis: Selected Papers of Lawrence S. Kubie.* Introduction by Eugene B. Brody

No. 45/46—Alan Krohn: *Hysteria: The Elusive Neurosis*

No. 47/48—Stanley I. Greenspan: *Intelligence and Adaptation: An Integration of Psychoanalytic and Piagetian Developmental Psychology*

No. 49—Gilbert J. Rose: *The Power of Form: A Psychoanalytic Approach to Aesthetic Form.* Foreword by Andrew Forge

No. 50—W. W. Meissner: *Internalization in Psychoanalysis*

PSYCHOLOGICAL ISSUES